THROW YOUR FEET OVER YOUR SHOULDERS

Beyond the Kindertransport

FRIEDA STOLZBERG KOROBKIN

DE**V**ORA

PUBLISHING

NEW YORK◆JERUSALEM◆LONDON

Throw Your Feet Over Your Shoulders:
Beyond the Kindertransport
Published by Devora Publishing Company
Copyright © 2008 Frieda Stolzberg Korobkin

COVER DESIGN: Benjie Herskowitz
TYPESETTING & BOOK DESIGN: Koren Publishing Services
EDITOR: Dvora Kiel
EDITORIAL & PRODUCTION MANAGER: Daniella Barak

Hard Cover ISBN: 978-1-934440-26-1

E-MAIL: sales@devorapublishing.com
WEB SITE: www.devorapublishing.com

Printed in the United States of America

For my children and grandchildren. And theirs...

The lights of heaven are your father and mother.

– Zohar

None can take the place reserved for martyrs in heaven.
– Talmud, Tractate Pesachim

CONTENTS

ACKNOWLEDGMENTS

Linda Hepner read a first draft of this memoir and her enthusiasm bucked me up when my own was flagging. Author Laura Waco took time from her own writing and film projects to read my manuscript; she made some very helpful suggestions and corrected my pitiable German. Author Sonia Levitin, too, was kind enough to read an early draft, and her encouragement buoyed me enormously. My dear friend Anita Wincelberg's advice and wisdom were, as always, my constant guides. My special thanks go to Rachelle Needle, who went through my manuscript with a fine-tooth comb on more than one occasion; I will be forever grateful for Rachelle's brilliant insights, masterful editing, and constructive suggestions.

My daughter, Jennifer, was unfailingly encouraging and supportive throughout the writing process. My sons, Rabbi Danny and Doc Sam, read early drafts and pointed out some glaring omissions, which I hope I have corrected adequately.

Dvora Kiel, my editor at Simcha Publishing, went beyond the call of duty in her conscientious editing of my manuscript. Her advice and suggestions were always illuminating and invaluable in achieving clarity of language and expression. Dvora: I cannot thank you sufficiently.

I owe a very special debt of gratitude to Yaakov Peterseil and Daniella Barak at Simcha, who gave me this opportunity to publish my story and helped me see the project through.

Acharon, acharon chaviv. Without the constant encouragement of my husband, Lenny, this memoir would never have seen the light of day. Thank you, Len, for your unfailing patience, good humor, support, and love.

FOREWORD

In December of 1938, nine months after the annexation of Austria by Germany, the *Anschluss*, my parents put their four children on a train in Vienna and sent us off to an unknown future in England, with the full realization that they might never see us again. All through the turbulent first eight months of 1939, thousands of Jewish parents in Germany, Austria, and Czechoslovakia packed their children off in similar fashion, until September 1, when Germany invaded Poland and, two days later, England declared war on Germany. Immediately, the Nazis put a halt to the children's transports. In all, ten thousand children were saved from an almost certain death through these *Kindertransports*, as they came to be known.

The torment and anguish suffered by those parents who were able to wrench themselves away from their children in this tragic manner, while others were unable to do so, is something that I cannot even begin to contemplate. For me, the *Kindertransports* evoke the biblical tale of the baby Moses whose mother, in an effort to save his life, launched him in a seaworthy basket on the

River Nile, not knowing what fate would befall him. (On a personal level, I find it ironic that Moses' mother and my mother shared the same name: Yocheved.)

Many accounts have been written about the *Kindertransports*. However there is one aspect of that undertaking that is not as well known as it deserves to be, and that is the almost single-handed rescue of one thousand – of the ten thousand children who were saved – by one man: Rabbi Solomon Schonfeld. All accounts I have read about the *Kindertransports* tell of Jewish children who had been reared in secular homes, who, like their parents, were thoroughly assimilated into the surrounding culture. In these pages I have attempted to describe the impact of the *Kindertransport* experience on children from Orthodox homes. Most of the one thousand children rescued by Rabbi Schonfeld came from observant backgrounds. As a result their culture shock was greater and their subsequent integration into British life was far more traumatic than for those children who had been used to eating nonkosher food in their own homes, had attended school with gentiles, and had rarely seen the inside of a synagogue.

In particular I have devoted the longest section of this work to Shefford, the village in England to which Rabbi Schonfeld's Jewish day school was transplanted in its entirety at the outbreak of the war. I believe this to be the first account of the unique Shefford experience seen through the eyes of a former student.

Initially I undertook this project as a personal memoir, as a legacy to my children and grandchildren. However as more and more memories came flooding back to me, and in talking to other old "Sheffordians," I realized that this important part of Holocaust history deserves to be recorded and preserved, not only for its own sake but as a tribute to the man to whom so many of us and our offspring owe our very existence: the late Rabbi Solomon Schonfeld, of blessed memory.

CHAPTER ONE

VIENNA

Vienna. The one and only. *Wien, Wien, nur du allein*. Even the song proclaims it, so it must be true. Vienna. The very name evokes echoes of Strauss waltzes and polkas, mischievous operettas, images of romantic trysts in lantern-strung woods, cafés and salons bursting with gaiety and intellectual discourse over plates of *Sachertorte* and *Apfelstrudel* and cups of coffee brimming with *Schlag*. Vienna. The city of Freud and Herzl. Both Jews, of course. Vienna. The city of so many infamous Jew-haters. Of course. And, eternally, Vienna, the city of the Danube, *Die Donau*, meandering through its canals and waterways, serenely unaware of the drama, the history, the tragedies playing out on its shores. The Danube, so tranquil and innocent. So blue, so blue.

The Vienna of my childhood contained no waltzes or polkas, no romantic visions, either real or imagined. And I would be very surprised to learn that the famous Vienna Woods or Schönbrunn Palace were ever honored with a visit from a member of my immediate family. One of my first vivid recollections, chilling in every sense, is being buried in the snow by three of Hitler's young hooligans.

It is winter 1938, a winter that is particularly harsh. I am not quite six years old. The pavement outside our apartment building is piled high with mounds and mounds of snow, which loom over my brother Ephraim and me like mountains. The two of us are having a fine old time, throwing snowballs and trying to build a snowman. The day is cold and crisp but sunny, under a cloudless sky. Other children down the street and across the way are also playing in the snow, and we in our blissful, childish innocence are not in the least concerned with the storm troopers, who just months before goose-stepped their way into the city to triumphant shouts of *Sieg Heil.*

One of Ephraim's snowballs misses me and hits a passing youth, a blond, blue-eyed boy of about twelve or thirteen wearing the *de rigueur* black jackboots and armband with its hypnotic insignia, a symbol that has become more and more familiar with each passing day. He is a perfect poster boy for the Hitler Youth. Before we know it, he and two of his friends, angry and menacing, have us surrounded and pinned down by the shoulders so we can't run away. "Where do you live?" they want to know. A mute Ephraim points a shaking finger at the building behind us. "Very well," sneers the first boy, the one insulted by the wayward snowball. "You go up to your Jewish mother and get us some chocolate. Meanwhile we will be having some fun with your little sister, and if you're not down by the count of one hundred, who knows what will happen to her."

My memory of what happened after that remains hazy. I remember the children across the street staring, and my best friend Rochel Ginzburg and her sister running into their building. Except that Rochel isn't my best friend anymore because yesterday in kindergarten she was a pest and so I spat into her spinach. I feel very cold and wet as they pile the snow over my head and some of it runs down my back. But then I become very warm and sleepy. I just want to sleep and sleep and sleep. As if from a great distance I hear the boys' laughter, the clanging of a tramcar, and then someone counting: *Eins, zwei, drei...*

We lived in a small flat at Heinzelmangasse 20 in the Twentieth *Bezirk*, which was a much poorer neighborhood than the predominantly Jewish Second *Bezirk*. In the Second *Bezirk* lived some middle-class Jews such as the Reichmans, whose apartment on the Taborstrasse was just around the corner from our Stolzberg grandparents' flat at Glockengasse 6, and not far from our Greisman cousins who lived near the Prater. Opa Shmuel and Oma Blima had been quite well off before World War 1 when they lived in Kolomea, Galicia, a part of Poland that was always changing hands and was, at that time, part of the Austro-Hungarian Empire. There, Opa owned a sweets factory and had many employees and peddlers working for him, among them Stephen Klein who founded Bartons Candies in the United States many years later. After the Great War, a time of galloping inflation ensued when paper money became practically worthless and, legend has it, people walked around with suitcases full of it just to buy a loaf of bread. While sugar had been the means by which Opa built his fortune, it was also the means of his economic downfall. In an effort to recoup his losses, Opa made some bad investments in sugar futures, and when the bottom fell out of the sugar market, he was left almost penniless. However he seemed to have had enough resources left to move his family to Vienna, into a decent apartment in a decent Jewish neighborhood.

That I didn't suffocate or freeze to death at the hands of the three young hooligans is self-evident. But there were several miracles attached to my rescue and survival, the first being that we lived just one flight up and so Ephraim had little distance to cover. The second miracle was that there was someone home, for often Oma Perl, who lived with us, would be down in the grocery shop helping Mama, but on that day Oma was home because it was Thursday and she was cooking for Shabbos. The third miracle was that when Oma opened the door to my brother's frantic knocking and was finally able to understand him, she actually had a few bars of milk chocolate in the flat. Usually chocolate was reserved as a special treat only for our birthdays. Once Oma grasped the critical nature of Ephraim's rescue mission, she pressed a bar of the precious chocolate into his hands and urged him frantically to hurry, "*Schnell, schnell, mach schnell mein Kind.*" And the last miracle was that my brave nine-year-old brother actually came back to rescue me at all.

*   *   *

My father, Nissan, was the elder son and the second of five children. He had an older sister, my Tante Regina, and a younger brother, Onkel Aaron. After Onkel Aaron came two much younger sisters, Tante Rosa and Tante Hanni, the rebels of the family. Both Rosa and Hanni wanted nothing to do with religion; they were self-declared agnostics, although both married Jewish men and were fervent Zionists.

Hanni was also a zealous Communist, a member of the party, and after the *Anschluss* she and her "fellow traveler," husband Edgar Neumann, fled to Argentina. Rosa's husband, Benno Ehrlich, held a fairly high position with the *Judische Kultusgemeinde* (Jewish Federation). His job allowed him to send Rosa to England right after the *Anschluss* but not before he had forced her to have an abortion. He declared that this was not a time to bring children into the world. As a result of this botched procedure, Rosa was never able to bear children.

Tante Regina and Onkel Pinchas had three daughters, Mina, Tonka, and Dorrit. In early 1938, nineteen-year-old Mina left for Palestine with her Gedonya youth group, and Tante Regina managed to smuggle Tonka and Dorrit into France, from where they eventually were able to reach America. Onkel Pinchas returned to Poland where his parents lived. As a devoted son he hoped to protect his parents from the coming onslaught. Neither he nor his parents were ever heard from again.

My father's younger brother, Aaron, was interned in Buchenwald toward the end of 1938. His ashes are buried in the Jewish cemetery in Vienna. His wife, Tante Frieda, landed in

Auschwitz in 1944 after having had to abandon her two young sons, Felix and Alexander, aged ten and twelve, on the streets of Budapest, where they scavenged for food and shelter. Their lives were saved by Raoul Wallenberg, who hid them in one of his safe houses. Fortunately, the boys' mother survived and they were reunited after the war.

The rivalry between Tante Regina and Tante Rosa was so intense that it became the stuff of family legend, sometimes to be ruefully laughed about but more often to be deplored. Regina was ten years older than Rosa, and when she married Onkel Pinchas, Opa was still able to give her a generous dowry. By the time Rosa's turn came to marry, Opa's fortune had dwindled, leaving Rosa sour and angry for the rest of her life. At times Rosa would accuse Regina of being the "*gonif* who stole my inheritance." At other times she would say bitterly, "Silver like that [or linen or china or crystal] shouldn't be found in the hands of peasants." It didn't help matters that Regina had three beautiful daughters while Rosa had been denied children in a most tragic manner. Depending on her mood, Regina might retaliate, sometimes very cruelly. "Murderer," she once screamed at Rosa, "at least I didn't kill my own children!"

Regina was jealous of Rosa's looks, for Rosa was the prettiest of the three sisters in a doll-like sort of way, which was why our grandparents and Onkel Benno called her *Puppe*. She had a neat, compact figure and always dressed elegantly despite her financial limitations. She favored pastel colors for the summer: pink and sky blue, and green to match her eyes. In the winter she wore smart woolen suits with fur collars, high-heeled suede shoes that showed off her shapely legs, and jaunty hats with sprouting feathers. By contrast, Regina was a big, unshapely woman with the trademark Stolzberg nose and little fashion sense. On many occasions Regina deliberately stoked the fires of Rosa's jealousy. After Benno sent Rosa to England, there were whispered rumors linking him romantically with a widow who had taken lodgings in my grandparents' flat. When Regina discovered them *in flagrante delicto*, she wrote to Rosa about the whole torrid affair. Rosa insisted that Benno leave Vienna immediately and join her in England, which he did, with his tail between his legs, just before the war broke out in earnest, thus probably saving his life. Though naturally, Tante Regina was not given the credit for it.

*   *   *

I have a recurring dream. Or perhaps it is a real memory, I'm not sure. I am walking with Papa. Except I am not really walking but floating on air beside him. A joyous constriction rises in my throat and threatens to choke off my breathing. Papa is holding my hand tightly, as if he will never let me go. We make our way toward the park that leads down to the river. I am carrying a brown paper bag filled with salt with which I intend to salinate the Danube. Somewhere I've heard that salt water keeps people afloat even if they are unable to swim, and I'm determined to make the Danube buoyant for nonswimmers like myself. In Papa's free hand he carries the thick, heavy tome that accompanies him wherever he goes. Today I have no mother, no sisters, no brother. There is just Papa and me: Papa in his long, black coat and hat despite the balmy weather, the fine lines of his forehead standing out like auxiliary roads on a country map; and I in the faded cotton frock that has known two sisters before me, and on my feet brown shoes that lace right up past my ankles and are so old and cracked that they resemble the faces of two ninety-year-old grandfathers.

We sit on the grass verge leading down to the water and I begin sprinkling the river with salt. A pleasure boat cruises along on a late summer outing, throwing up little waves in its wake that wash up on the shore and reach almost to our feet. Lively music blares from the vessel and carries to our spot. Papa's thumb is arrested halfway into its nosedive over the open page. He turns to me and, surprisingly, he is talking about genies. *Friedl*, he asks, *what would you wish for if a genie were suddenly to appear?* I don't have to think. I clap my hands and say, *Oh, half-shoes, Papa, half-*

shoes. Then I'll be just like the Ginzburg girls, the only girls on our street with half-shoes. Papa throws back his head and laughs, revealing the two crooked bottom teeth that overlap. And I realize suddenly that I've not seen or heard him laugh like that for quite a while. He pats me on the head and continues smiling. He just pats me on the head and smiles.

After my brush with the Hitler Youth, Oma takes me into her bed to warm me up while Ephraim, also shaken from the experience, curls up on one of the other beds and goes to sleep. Oma makes sure to hold me against her good side. Her bad side, which was injured years before when a cyclist collided with her, gives her so much pain that sometimes the neighbors complain because of her screams. Today is one of her better days, and I'm able to snuggle up against her under the soft down bedding until I am thoroughly thawed out. Then, dressed in dry clothes, I follow Oma into the kitchen, where sheets of dough are hanging to dry over the backs of chairs, waiting for her to roll them up and slice them for *lokshen* and strudel. I sit at Oma's feet, holding on to her good leg, while she grates chocolate into a bowl to be sprinkled over the semolina we are to have for supper, as a special treat. Every now and then she lets some shavings drop by accident on purpose into my waiting mouth. It soon becomes a game. Two strokes into the bowl, the third into my open mouth. With each delicious capture, I laugh with glee and hug Oma's leg even tighter. I rub my cheek against the worn leather of her shoes, which seem merely to be an extension of her body. The leather carries her unique smell, a curious yet pleasing mixture of lavender water and yeast, for Oma bakes so often that the aroma clings to everything she wears. Oma is small and frail and with each passing day seems to shrink more and more into herself. I'm afraid she will soon disappear. Today, as every day, she's wearing her old brown cardigan that is so frayed and moth-eaten, especially at the elbows, that it reminds me of the cheese with holes that Mama sells by the slice in the shop. The cardigan cannot possibly provide

7

much warmth anymore. I continue caressing and kissing Oma's leg; I even kiss her high-laced shoes. *You silly goose*, she says to me. *You silly goose.*

That is what she calls me. You silly goose.

Oma, Oma, when they came for you, was it day or night? Was it hot or cold? Was your hip bothering you? Were you wearing that old brown cardigan with the threadbare elbows? What were you feeling? What were you thinking? And when they tossed you like a piece of refuse onto the lorry, forgive me, Oma, for wondering if any thought of your Friedl, your silly goose, entered your head. And later, when they crammed you into the cattle car, did you think back to how you used to swing me on your lap, singing "Hoppa hoppa Reiter" or how you used to lull me to sleep with "Rozhinkes und Mandeln"? Did you recall how Mama and Papa went on holiday to Baden taking Erika and Mimi and Ephraim with them, but left me at home with you because they couldn't trust me not to wet the bed in the hotel? How you comforted me with chocolate treats and sang "Oif dem Pripichik" over and over again?

Forgive me, Oma, for inserting myself into your tragedy, for trespassing on your nightmare. But you see, I'm tortured by not knowing.

And when you reached your final destination, my Oma, when you reached that evil place whose name I cannot bring past my lips, were you already unable to feel or think? Were you by then mercifully oblivious to your surroundings, to what was being done to you?

How I pray it was so. Oh Oma! How I pray it was so.

* * *

Our apartment is a dismal affair, a cold-water flat consisting of three rooms, of which Oma shares one with Papa's overflowing bookshelves. There is an eat-in kitchen and one large all-purpose room in which all six of us sleep. Off the kitchen is a small lavatory and sink. Because I still wet my bed, nobody wants to sleep with me, but Mama makes sure to rotate us so everyone gets a turn. On Thursday nights, all of us children bathe, one by one, in a wooden tub, which is kept under the kitchen table when not in use and filled with water heated on the stove. After we have bathed, Mama cuts our nails. When she's finished, she carefully gathers all the clippings onto a piece of paper, which she then folds and throws into the stove to be burnt.

My parents are always worried about my oldest sister, Erika, who is fifteen. Something is not quite right with Erika, or as Mama often says sadly in Yiddish, "*Es fehlt ihr eppes.*" Apart from German, Yiddish is what we speak most often. When my parents and Oma don't want us to understand, they speak Polish. Mama despairs of curing Erika of some of her disgusting habits. Indeed, there is something "missing" in Erika, something not quite right. For instance, Erika insists on eating with her fingers, totally ignoring the fork or spoon at the side of her plate. To sit with her at the supper table can ruin the healthiest appetite. On bath nights, Mama tries to get Erika to take her bath first because it takes so long to get her into the tub. On the way there she gets sidetracked by a daydream or a question she has to ask Oma, or something she has to look at urgently, perhaps a scratch on her leg that has to be pondered and examined and analyzed. Even after Mama manages to get her into the tub, it takes more reminders and threats to get her to wash her hair, something she loathes doing, and more nagging and prodding to get her to come out. When Mama tries to get Erika to help with household chores, no sooner is her back turned than Erika stops sweeping or dusting or washing dishes and stares out the window, humming dreamily, totally oblivious to Mama's reprimands, which sail over her head, unheard and invisible, like clouds over a blind man.

On the other hand, much like an idiot savant, Erika has one quality for which all her disturbing habits are temporarily forgotten. She has a soprano voice so sweet and pure that, listening to her, even Herr Hitler's heart must melt. On Friday nights, after Papa and Ephraim come home from the *shtiebel*, our little flat becomes for a few hours a scene of perfect domestic harmony. For those few hours my parents push all stress aside, and the goose-stepping world outside our little haven ceases to exist. Our eyes and faces glow in the candlelight, and the flickering shadows thrown off by the Shabbos candles turn the flaking walls, bare floors, and rag-shrouded windows of our room into an exotic chamber. Just before Shabbos, my sister Mimi brushed and combed my hair until it shone, and tied it back with a white ribbon. We are all wearing our best clothes, most of which were handed down from our Greisman and Horowitz cousins.

After Papa blesses each of us, after the *Kiddush* and *Motzi,* after the fish has been eaten and the soup plates taken away and our bellies are filled with chicken, *lokshen kugel,* and *tzimmes,* Papa pushes back his chair, draws Ephraim and me onto each knee, and clears his throat. "Nu, Esterle," he says, using the diminutive of Erika's Hebrew name, "Are you ready?" Then, in his strong, true baritone, he begins one of the special Shabbos *nigunim,* and Erika joins in carrying the melody while Papa slips into the harmony, underscoring Erika's soprano. A shiver of happiness runs through me when their voices blend and soar and travel throughout the whole building and out into the courtyard. I imagine their voices spiraling all the way up to the gates of heaven where the angels dwell. Where the angels dwell and weep with joy.

After we have *bentched,* Papa perches me on his shoulders and stands with his back against the warm tiles of the blue ceramic stove in the corner of the room. The stove reaches all the way up to the ceiling and is our only source of heat. Then he begins to relate the weekly Torah portion, spinning tales of ancient heroes and villains, bringing to life our biblical ancestors. I can't make up my mind which story is my favorite: the splitting of the Red Sea or the one about Joseph and his coat of many colors.

"Papa," I ask, "what did the coat look like? How many colors were in it? How long was it? Did it have a fur collar? Who sewed it?"

If I close my eyes and concentrate, I can still hear Papa's voice. "Well, Friedl, let's see. It was probably made of different squares, like a quilt. There was red and blue, yellow and green, purple and..." But by this time, my head is nodding drowsily on his shoulder....

Another memory. My favorite cousin, Fritz Horowitz, has come to say goodbye. He is leaving for America. It must have been a Thursday night, because I'm sitting in the wooden tub getting my weekly bath. I am still too young to be embarrassed. I barely recognize him. Fritz has always been tall, but now he's painfully thin, which makes him look even taller, and his head has been shaved; there is just a light bristle where his hair is starting to grow in again. Fritz has just been released from a place called Dachau, where the Nazis kept him for six weeks until he was able to prove that he had papers allowing him to leave the country. Fritz relates how he was able to get his exit visa. His story is both tragic and uplifting at the same time.

Some months before the Germans marched into Vienna, Fritz and his younger brother Josef acted as sightseeing guides for two American spinster school teachers. Even gentile tourists enjoying a holiday in Vienna must have been aware of the war clouds gathering over Europe and that the situation was becoming especially difficult for Jews. Before they returned to America, the ladies offered to sponsor the boys should they ever wish to emigrate to the United States. After the *Anschluss*, true to their word, the ladies sent the boys affidavits. Alas, seventeen-year-old Josef was never able to use his affidavit. He was attacked by a mob of Hitler Youth as he was crossing the street; they kicked and beat him so badly that his kidneys failed and he died of his wounds. Fritz is the son of Onkel David, Mama's brother; his family is assimilated and not at all religious, but Fritz feels a close connection to my mother, his Tante Yocheved, which is why he has come to say goodbye.

I am impatient for Fritz to finish his story because I want to show him my loose tooth. Finally I have his attention. I open my mouth and wiggle the tooth with my finger. This is my first loose tooth and I am very excited. I tell Fritz how Papa wanted to tie a piece of string around it and attach the other end of the string to a doorknob, and then yank the door shut so as to pull the tooth out, but I wouldn't let him. Fritz looks into my mouth and admires the loose tooth to my satisfaction. Before he leaves he kisses me on the head and tells me to be sure to put the tooth under my pillow after it comes out. He says this will bring me luck.

*   *   *

It was quite obvious to Opa Shmuel that not only did his eldest son have no interest in making money, he possessed not one ounce of business acumen. All Papa ever wanted to do was study Torah. And so, at a very early age, he was packed off to various yeshivas, culminating with the prestigious yeshiva of Vizhnitz, where he received his *semichah*, his rabbinical ordination. At some point during the Great War, Papa's yeshiva studies were rudely interrupted by an invitation from the Austrian army. Just thinking about Papa in uniform, marching with a rifle on his shoulder, makes me smile. Fortunately Papa's military career was short-lived. There was no kosher food to be had in the army and Papa went on a hunger strike. His superiors threw up their hands in disgust and sent him home!

After his less-than-honorable discharge from the Austrian army, a marriage was arranged, a *shidduch*, between my father, whose reputation for Jewish scholarship was by then established, and the daughter of the Chassidic grand rabbi of Stanislav, Rav Ephraim Fishel Horowitz, scion of one of the many branches of the famous and far-flung Horowitz dynasty that traces its roots back to the revered medieval biblical commentator, the holy Shelah and, some say, all the way back to King David himself. It was considered the perfect match: the beautiful daughter of an important rabbi and the learned prodigy, son of a (still) wealthy merchant. My mother had the added but controversial cachet of having been allowed some kind of informal secular education, something unheard of in Chassidic circles. As a result, she not only had read books that were generally forbidden to Orthodox Jewish girls but, in addition to speaking Polish, German and Yiddish, had a smattering of several languages including English and French. She also had developed a deep appreciation for music, especially Strauss waltzes, which she loved. This anomaly might have proved an obstacle to the match rather than an advantage had my mother's pedigree, her *yichus*, not been so impeccable in every other respect and had she not possessed such remarkable looks. Mama was the talk of her milieu: in today's parlance, a "catch." (Many years later in New York, I met a woman who had known my parents in Vienna and who confirmed to me that Mama, with her strawberry-blonde hair, blue eyes, and porcelain skin, had been exquisite. The woman then turned to me, looked me up and down, and announced, "But of course my dear, you take after your father!")

I suspect that Oma was the force behind her daughter's unusual education. For Oma was quite a rebel herself and was suspected of sneaking a smoke in the lavatory when she thought no one was looking. I never knew Opa Ephraim Fishel, who died long before my brother or I were born; in fact my brother was named for him.

My father was a quiet, contemplative man, an impractical man, a dreamer, an idealist and a poet. A man of perfect faith who had an absolute, unquestioning trust in his Maker's design for the Jewish people in general, and for his own family in particular. All of these traits are clearly manifested in the only *sefer* Papa managed to write before the world closed in on him. He called his book, which is a commentary on the first chapter of *Pirkei Avot* (*Ethics of the Fathers*), *Sefer He'Aviv* (*The Book of Spring*), an oblique reference to his name, Nissan, which is also the name of the Jewish month associated with the beginning of the spring season.

Papa's favorite saying was *Gott wird helfen*, "God will help." When Opa Shmuel lost all his money and was no longer able to help his children, Papa said, *Gott wird helfen*. When Mama miscarried her first few pregnancies, he said, *Gott wird helfen.* When Hitler's rumblings were heard in the early thirties and the family's economic situation became ever more dire, Papa continued to say *Gott wird helfen.* And Papa was right. Help came in the form of Mama who, suppressing her own impractical nature and with Oma's help, opened a grocery shop on Heinzelmangasse just down the street from our flat and a few doors away from Papa's *shtiebel.* The shop catered to our Jewish neighbors and not only was it our economic salvation, it held our hunger at bay even when our neighbors were beginning to starve.

In theory, Papa was supposed to help out in the shop. Reality told a different story. Papa and his Talmudic tome would retire behind the curtained partition at the back of the counter together with a glass of hot tea and some sugar cubes. Once comfortably ensconced, he was transported to another world. When the shop filled up with customers, out of desperation Mama would call, *Nissan, Nissan, ich bitte dich,* "Please, I beg you," and if he heard her he would heave a great sigh of regret, gently close his book, and emerge slowly from behind the curtain with a slightly dazed look, much like a modest performer reluctant to take a bow. More often than not, Papa's concentration was so complete that he was deaf to Mama's calls for assistance. Then Oma was sent for and would come limping down, hastily wiping her hands on her apron and mumbling benign imprecations under her breath about her useless son-in-law. Yet, if it were possible, Oma loved her son-in-law even more than she loved her own daughter. For Oma was ever mindful that her presence in her children's cramped living quarters deprived them of privacy. The courtesy and consideration my father invariably showed his mother-in-law did not spring from affection alone; it arose also from a conscious desire and effort to have his every action reflect the precepts outlined in the codex by which he lived: the holy Torah.

I have a black-and-white photograph of my father, the only photograph that has survived. It is a copy of a copy. In it he is wearing a dark suit and tie and a dapper homburg. His auburn beard appears black, and he is gazing dully through black-rimmed spectacles directly into the eye of the camera. Over his left arm is suspended the handle of a furled umbrella and in his right hand he holds something conical in shape, perhaps a rolled-up newspaper. The provenance of the photograph is unknown, and though it is impossible to tell Papa's exact age, he appears to be in his mid thirties, which would date the photograph at just a few years before the *Anschluss*. Perhaps the sadness I detect in my father's eyes is a product of my imagination. But it seems to me that his eyes contain a deep bewilderment, a rudely blunted innocence. As if he cannot quite believe what is happening to his life, to his people, to his world.

Of my mother, no photographs have survived.

*   *   *

Papa is chasing me around the table, his voice raised to an unaccustomed level of anger. *This is the last straw,* he says. *The absolute last straw.* I run to Oma for protection, but even Oma will not help me on this occasion. What have I done? I have been discovered playing with Inge again, the daughter of our apartment building's janitor. As if this isn't bad enough – because I have been strictly forbidden to play with the *shiksa* – to make matters worse I have confessed that I ate a piece of Inge's mother's freshly baked *streusel Kuchen.* I have eaten *treif.* And to pile sin upon sin, I have defiantly declared that it was delicious! In the past, I've heard my parents talk about the janitor and his wife in very uncomplimentary terms. *Those anti-Semites,* I once overhead Mama say, *they should be struck down by a plague.* Papa drags me out from under the bed and keeps spanking me until I promise never to play with Inge again. This is not the first time I have been spanked, nor the first time I have made the same promise.

A visit to Opa Shmuel and Oma Blima is a rare treat, especially as we often find Tante Regina and our three Greisman cousins there and they always make a big fuss over me. My grandparents' flat is comfortably furnished with the ghosts of Opa's lost fortune: carpets and draperies, and deep, soft armchairs, all luxurious accouterments that are as foreign to us as the delicacies Oma Blima serves on our visits.

Oma Blima stands over us, her eyes alight with pleasure, as we stuff ourselves with roasted meats and exotic fruits such as bananas and pineapples and strawberries. And, best of all, Oma Blima's specialty: chocolate balls rolled in grated coconut. Like Proust and his famous madeleines, I can, in my memory, taste them still, and they conjure up an elusive, shadowy vision of Oma Blima that skitters around in my head: a compact, neat woman, with a short, dark brown *sheitel*, lively brown eyes, and nervous hands that are never still.

My memory of Opa Shmuel with his grey beard, prominent Stolzberg nose, and gentle hands is more solid. Opa Shmuel has a reputation for piety and modesty. So modest is he that when he walks outside he keeps his eyes firmly fixed to the ground. As a result, he very often finds items of value. Or so he says. For it is quite amazing the things he claims to have "found" lying in the gutters of Vienna. Sometimes money, sometimes a toy. Even more remarkable is how appropriate each find is: once a red leather purse for Erika and some fancy ribbons for Mimi's golden ringlets. And once, most amazing, not one, but two identical yo-yos for Ephraim and me, yo-yos that are painted in all the colors of the rainbow and ride magically up and down the string with barely any effort on our part at all.

*   *   *

Opa Shmuel is one of the first to be taken. We grimly surmise his fate. Oma Blima opens the door to two jackbooted Nazis wearing swastika armbands and clicking their heels in sardonic courtesy. One of them carries a small cardboard box. *Gnadige Frau*, they greet her sarcastically. *Wir haben ihnen ein Geschenk gebracht.* "Dear lady, we have brought you a present." With that they march right past her, not wishing to defile themselves by physical contact with a Jewess, and place the box on the mantel. With another exaggerated click of the heels, they depart.

Oma Blima opens the box. It is filled with ashes.

December. It is cold. A bone-eroding cold both inside and out. There is no more heat in our flat, and Papa sits, no, crouches over his book day and night, swaying to and fro, to and fro, his overcoat never leaving his back. He drinks endless glasses of hot tea, and when his hands are not wrapped around the warm glass they rub each other in a steady washing motion in his lap. Our school, the Talmud Torah Schule, in which Mimi, Ephraim, and I are enrolled and where Papa teaches, has been closed by the Nazis. The *Gymnasium* Erika goes to is no longer allowing Jewish children to attend. As a result, the four of us have been confined to our three little rooms for weeks. The flat has begun to feel like a prison. My sisters, my brother, and I play our games in half-hearted fashion, desultorily. Even our squabbles lack enthusiasm. One day last week, one of the neighbors warned that there would be a "roundup" of men, but that only the healthy ones were to be taken. Hurriedly, Mama coaxes Papa into bed and by some miracle somehow manages to raise his temperature, so that he looks and feels really hot and ill. I am given some wads of paper money to hide in my thick stockings. Surely they will not search a mere child? There is a loud pounding on the door. *Aufmachen*, a voice orders, and two men in the dreaded black uniforms and armbands force their way into the flat and start tossing our belongings around the room. All of us stand as if in a tableau, except Papa who is "sick" in bed. When they establish that the man of the house is really ill, they leave in disgust, but not before breaking some crockery and cursing the *verfluchte Juden*.

The next time we are not so lucky. It is Friday night and Papa is about to make *Kiddush*, when, without warning, they once again burst into our flat. This time, they order my parents and our Jewish neighbors downstairs, force them onto their hands and knees, and make them scrub the streets. After that, the hoodlums break into Papa's *shtiebel*, seize the Torah scrolls and prayer books, and throw them onto a huge bonfire out in the middle of the street, to the loud cheers of our gentile neighbors. And none cheer more loudly than our janitor and his wife and my friend Inge.

They also close our grocery shop. First they break the windows, then they ransack the shelves. My parents are forced to sweep up the broken glass and debris. There is no more food left. Each morning, Mama and Erika leave the house, each of them carrying a saucepan. They queue up outside the Jewish community center for the daily food ration. Each day they creep home a little more weary and silent than the day before and climb fully clothed into one bed, where they hold onto each other for warmth. Ephraim and I climb in, too, fighting for a place next to Mama. Fighting to get on top of her, under her, inside her. Back inside her womb.

Nein, nein, nein, Nissan, nein! screams my mother, and then disintegrates into convulsive sobs. More and more often lately, my sleep has been interrupted by loud arguments between my parents who, until now, always have spoken to each other in quiet tones. Tonight, as usual, they are talking about *die Kinder*. Actually, this time, it is only Mama's voice that is raised. Papa speaks softly, resignedly, sadly. *Es muss so sein, Yocheved*, he says. *Es muss so sein.* "It must be so." He adds, "It is not in our hands. *Gott wird helfen.*"

My father's faith in God was once again rewarded. This time, help came from a stranger, a young rabbi in England. My father had heard that this young man, Rabbi Solomon Schonfeld, with the assistance of the Agudah organization in London, was arranging to bring groups of children out of Austria, Germany, and Czechoslovakia to the safety of Holland and England. My father acquired places on one of the transports for all four of us, insisting that we be assigned to a group going all the way to England.

He was very clear about not wishing our final destination to be Holland. God must have endowed him with prophetic vision, for Papa's foresight probably saved our lives.

*   *   *

We are told that we are embarking on a great adventure, first by train and then by boat. Until now the only vehicle I have ever ridden in is a tramcar, and so I am very excited. I have been warned to be on my best behavior and to obey my eleven-year-old sister, Mimi, who will be in charge of me on the journey.

"Don't worry, *Kinder*, we will join you soon," my parents tell us.

"When?" we want to know.

"We don't know exactly when, perhaps in a few weeks or a few months. But we will see you soon. Everything will be all right. You will see. Just be good and do what you are told." Then they tell us about the wonderful young rabbi who will be there to greet us and take care of us until they arrive and we can be together again.

When the time comes for Papa to take us to the railway station, I can't understand why Oma and Mama are making such a fuss. After all, they will be joining us soon. My last clouded memory of Mama is seeing her holding Oma up, or perhaps it is the other way around, as they sob uncontrollably in each other's arms.

It is very cold outside and the streets are still covered with snow. Once again, Papa is holding my hand, but this time I don't feel the actual flesh of his fingers, just the long, bony outlines, for my hands are protected by mittens, which are attached to each other by a long string drawn through my coat sleeves and around my neck. Papa's hands, too, are encased in gloves, but once again his grip is hard and tight as if he will never let me go. He has forsaken his book for an old, brown leather suitcase, which is miraculously held together by an apologetic piece of string and Mama's prayers.

It is a long time since I have been outside and I am not used to the bright lights and Christmas decorations that are everywhere. There are large posters and flags hanging from every window displaying the swastika and the picture of a funny-looking man with a funny little mustache. I stretch my neck in all directions, taking it all in, and do not notice the two thugs in brown shirts and black boots until they are upon us. They throw Papa up against a wall, and he jerks me after him. There is a flash of steel, and then his beard is no longer there. Just a jagged red mess attached to his chin. Laughter. I cannot move. My legs are frozen to the spot just as they were one afternoon a few months ago when, on entering our building after playing with my friends, a man jumped out at me from the shadows and tried to thrust his hand up my skirt. The armbands with their compelling, invincible insignia have a hypnotic effect on me. I can't take my eyes from them. More laughter. Erika and Mimi and Ephraim are also rooted to the spot, transfixed like statues, staring in disbelief.

Silently, we continue on our way. Not once has Papa uttered a sound. I peer up at him. His lip is bleeding, his face has taken on the hue of cold ashes. The yellow street lights reflect ghoulishly in his eyes, which stare sightlessly ahead. My hand stays glued to his, his to mine.

The chaos at the Westbahnhof was a scene that lives forever in my memory. Yet I cannot find words to describe it adequately. Parents and children clung and tore at each other and gazed into each other's eyes for what they knew might be the last time, desperately trying to store each feature in their memory banks. Above the harsh clackety-clack of locomotives arriving and departing, above the train whistles, above the shrieking of brakes and hissing of steam, there rose wave upon wave of anguish that formed itself into a primeval wail that had no beginning and no end. Like some monstrous, mortally wounded beast in its final throes of agony. Was it at that moment that it dawned on me that perhaps this might not be such a wonderful adventure after all? Is that why, when the time came to board the train, my father had to force me kicking and screaming into the carriage? I was so angry with him that I refused to look at him again or wave goodbye from the train window, despite Mimi's urging. As a result, I am haunted forever by the image of my father standing desolate and bleeding on that station platform, watching helplessly as the train carrying his four children vanished before his eyes.

Dearest Papa, what did you feel when you saw the train disappear into the tunnel? Were you angry with me? Disappointed? Did you want to run after the train and drag us all off the way that other father did who snatched his daughter from the compartment just as the train began to move? What happened when you arrived home? Had Mama and Oma stopped crying? What did they say when they saw your bleeding face without its beard? What did you tell them?

The train is having a hard time getting through the snow. It plows forward a few yards, then churns back. Forward and then back again. The snow flies off the wheels and hisses softly against the windows like myriads of tiny, whispering serpents. There are no men to clear the tracks. They are all serving in the army of the Third Reich and cannot be spared. Through the window, Austria and then Germany roll away in one vast glacial landscape. The Fatherland is pure and white and peaceful, entirely without menace. Mimi hugs me against her, not merely for comfort, but also for warmth, because the compartment is unheated. The other girls in the compartment are sobbing uncontrollably. Mimi tries to hold back her tears, but every now and then a sob escapes her. Boys and girls have been separated; Ephraim is in another part of the train, while Erika is with the older girls.

A lady comes around carrying cups containing a steaming, foul-smelling liquid. This is tea, we are told. English tea with milk. "Drink," she urges us, "it's nourishing and will warm your insides." We examine the strange mixture with suspicion. Tentatively, we take a sip, then shudder and grimace with disgust. Are they trying to poison us? After the lady leaves the compartment, one of the girls manages to open the window a crack and we slop the alien brew out onto the snow where brown stains immediately appear and spread over the white surface, then are swallowed up. It has taken only a moment, but in that short time, a gust of arctic air has entered our compartment, making it even more frigid than before. We stamp our feet and flap our arms around our bodies. One of the girls starts a song. Steam rises from our mouths to the swaying ceiling as we sing songs with Hebrew words that every-body knows. We sing "*Artzah Alinu.*" Then someone starts a song in German about a three-cornered hat. She is quickly hushed. We don't want to hear any more German. We are going to a new country where we will learn a new language.

In this painfully slow fashion our *Kindertransport* crosses from Germany into Holland. A journey that normally takes hours has taken more than a day. What started as an exciting adventure has lost its appeal. As soon as we cross the Dutch border, everyone exhales deeply, as if we have been saving our breath until this mo-ment. Now we are safe. Safe to complain that we are cold, that we are tired, that we are hungry. Safe to cry for our mothers.

We are taken to a deserted school where kind ladies feed us a delicious hot meal. It is nice to be on firm land; it is nice not to be shaking from side to side, backward and forward; it is nice to be warm and fussed over. Perhaps the adventure will turn out well, after all. But where is the man our parents told us about? Where is this Pied Piper who is a foreigner but who nevertheless has such a comforting, *Umlaut*-sounding name? Where is this Rabbi Schonfeld? There is a commotion near the door. We all turn in that direction; the kind ladies have an adoring look in their eyes.

A man has entered, but to me he looks more like a giant than an ordinary man. Like the giants in the Bible stories Papa used to tell us on Friday nights. He is very tall and big and broad-shoul-dered, with a firm, strong stride, a ruddy beard, and an undulating voice that is craggy like mountain ridges. He is quite old, like Papa, forty at least. On the other hand, he seems quite young, ageless, in fact. His voice booms across the enormous room and immediately captures everyone's attention. He is speaking in German, but I don't listen to what he is saying and peer out at him fearfully from behind Mimi's skirt, where I have taken refuge. He begins to move around the room, pausing here and there to chat with some of the children. His mountainous laugh reverberates, making me quiver with apprehension.

"What is that behind your back?" the giant asks my sister, and at the same time shoots out his arm to pull me from my hiding place. "What have we here?" he thunders as I look fearfully up into his eyes, which are a disturbing shade of blue. But perhaps they are green. It is impossible to tell.

He bends down, and in a voice very grim inquires in German, "Can a little girl like you speak Yiddish?" Ah, I think to myself, you believe you have caught me, but I will show you. "Yes," I answer defiantly, no longer afraid. "Of course I speak Yiddish."

"Then say something," the giant commands, his eyes flashing, amused. I realize I must say something that will make this big giant go away. But what? And then I remember. My voice is steady and bold as I say to him, "Throw your feet over your shoulders and run away!"[1] And I almost stick out my tongue for good measure. The giant straightens up and throws back his head, his beard begins to wobble up and down, and then he lets out a gust of laughter that sends me back to my hiding place behind Mimi's skirt, for this is not the reaction I expected. Once more he stretches out his arm, but this time he draws me gently to his side.

"*Sehr gut,*" he says, holding me close to him, still laughing. "*Sehr gut, mein Yiddishe Maidele.*"

It is only then that I notice the large menorah standing on a

---

1. Transliterated in Yiddish: *Nem die fis oif die plaitzes und antlauf,* or as we'd say colloquially: Pack up your feet, throw them over your shoulders, and get out of here!

table in a corner of the room. It is the seventh night of Chanukah. We all crowd around the table and listen to Rabbi Schonfeld make the blessing and watch him light the candles. Then we sing "*Maoz Tzur*" together. Erika and Mimi and Ephraim and I stand close together, and Mimi holds my hand while we sing. I can't help wondering if Papa is also lighting Chanukah candles at this moment. And if he is, is it very lonely with just Mama and Oma there – and none of us to join in the singing?

CHAPTER TWO

LONDON

The overnight crossing from the Hook of Holland to Harwich is extremely rough and stormy. In addition to the blizzard, high winds are whipping up the waves, which, even from our cabin down below, can be heard crashing down onto the upper deck of the ship. Most of the children are violently seasick and the night is punctuated by sounds of retching and cries for Mama. Mimi and I share a cabin with some other girls. We all lie fully clothed on our bunks; Mimi has the bunk above mine. I am lucky. I'm the only one in our cabin not seasick. The constant tossing and shaking of the boat doesn't even frighten me; on the contrary, it lulls me to sleep. Mimi, on the other hand, is miserable, and her heaving and gagging wake me up.

"Please, Friedl," she says. "Please go and get me a slice of lemon." She says that a lemon will help her nausea. "Please," she begs, and her moans frighten me so much that I dash out of the cabin in stocking feet and run up and down the empty corridors in a frenzy. Where will I find a lemon in the middle of the night on a ship in a raging sea? Suddenly the vessel lurches over on its side and then, with a lot of shuddering and groaning of engines, rights itself again. I have been holding onto the bars attached to the corridor walls to prevent myself from falling and I'm afraid to let go. The corridors are deserted and quiet except for the sounds of misery coming from behind the closed cabin doors. Finally a sailor comes to my rescue and leads me by the hand to the galley, where another crewman cuts up a lemon and offers to take me back to my cabin.

"What is your cabin number, little girl?" he asks. Cabin number? What is that? All the doors look alike and there seem to be a million of them. Panic rises up in my throat as I try not to cry. Just then, as if by magic, the "giant" appears. He has been making the rounds of the cabins, comforting the seasick and homesick children. Rabbi Schonfeld takes my hand and leads me back to my cabin and my sister.

The following morning we land in England. It is snowing heavily and visibility is nil. The trains are not running and we will have to stay in Harwich, at least for one night. Rabbi Schonfeld's helpers are unprepared for this crisis. They accommodate our group of girls in an old abandoned coal cellar that still contains evidence of its former use. The coal dust seeps into our noses and throats, and settles into the folds of our bodies and clothes. There is very little in the way of food. The date is December 24. The shops are closed for the holidays, but even had they been open, they would be unlikely to contain many kosher items in a town that probably has seen very few, if any, Jews before now. Toward evening, from the street above the cellar, come sounds of laughter, singing, and merrymaking. Carolers making their rounds in the snow, spreading Yuletide cheer. We are each given an apple and some biscuits to assuage our hunger. I share a narrow mattress on the cold, sooty floor with Mimi, and we sleep with our coats on. She doesn't complain when I wet the bed.

The next day, conditions allow us to travel by train to

London's Victoria Station. We are loaded onto buses and get our first glimpse of a London shrouded in white: Waterloo Bridge, the River Thames, the Houses of Parliament, Big Ben. There are very few buses or cars on the roads, and the sky is still sending down bursts of snow flurries. I am too tired even to look out the window. I put my head on Mimi's shoulder and doze for most of the way. We have not seen Erika or Ephraim since we boarded the ship. They must be on a different bus. We alight in an area called Stamford Hill and are once again taken to a school where the large assembly hall has been converted into a dining room with long trestle tables and benches. There is a lot of noise and confusion as we all mill around, our knapsacks still fastened to our backs, identifying labels pinned to our coats, waiting to be told what to do. In all the chaos, we finally spot Erika and Ephraim, only to hear some devastating news. Ephraim is being shipped off to Cardiff, Wales, a city on the other side of the country, where he is to live in a hostel for boys. Erika, too, is leaving us, but she is going to Manchester, a town to the north, where she will live with Tante Regina who left Vienna before we did and has found work as a seamstress. Erika will be her assistant. Erika is thrilled to be joining a member of the family and doesn't mind at all parting from us.

Ephraim is stoic. "I am the man of the family now," he says, "and I am not allowed to cry." And, indeed, it is as if Ephraim has aged overnight. His back is straighter and he seems to have grown taller. Suddenly, he reminds me of Opa Shmuel, in the shape of his head and the *peyos*, the sidelocks, which are curled neatly behind his ears. At home he always wore them loose, fluttering wildly on his cheeks. To my amazement, he gives me a quick, almost embarrassed, hug. This is the first time there has been a display of affection between us. He promises to write to us as soon as he gets to Cardiff. It is only later that Mimi and I realize we have no idea how to contact him in Cardiff and that he may not know how to contact us either.

After we have eaten, Mimi and I, together with some other

girls, are taken by bus to a house on Lordship Park Road, where we are to sleep. The house has three levels and many rooms, each containing beds. Even the drawing room and dining room on the ground floor are lined with beds from wall to wall. There is a bathroom and lavatory on each floor, and every sink has hot and cold running water and something called a geyser in each bathroom to heat the bath water. We learn that Rabbi Schonfeld, who is not yet married, lives in this house with his mother but that she is away on holiday. His eyes alive with mischief, Rabbi Schonfeld tells us that his mother doesn't know that her furniture has been moved out of the house and replaced with beds and refugees. He rubs his hands gleefully. "She is certainly in for a big surprise when she returns," he says.

On the following morning some families come to adopt us, just temporarily, until our parents arrive to claim us. A friendly looking couple, Mr. and Mrs. Perlow, want to take Mimi home to live with them. They have a daughter Mimi's age for whom they would like a companion. Mimi tells them she can't go with them because she cannot be separated from her little sister. But the Perlows have room for only one little girl to share their daughter's bedroom. Another couple, Mr. and Mrs. Simmons, have been listening to this exchange. They offer to take me into their home. They have two sons, but their flat is larger than the Perlows' and I will have a room to myself. Mimi again says she doesn't wish to be separated from me. Rabbi Schonfeld takes things into his hands and decides for us. He must empty out his house to make room for another *Kindertransport*, which is due to arrive in a couple of days. And so the matter is settled.

*   *   *

Mr. and Mrs. Simmons own a dry cleaning shop on Commercial Road in the East End of London, in a district called Whitechapel. Their flat takes up two floors above the shop. Next door is a photographer's shop, over whose door hangs a large yellow and black Kodak sign. The Simmonses speak to me in a Yiddish that I can barely understand, and they, in turn, also have difficulty understanding me. I try out the English phrases Mama taught me, *Idontknow, thankyou, howareyou,* but they don't understand my English either. Mr. Simmons is a quiet, gentle man and only speaks to me when his wife is not in the room. He has blue eyes and wears glasses. One of his eyes is covered by a white, filmy substance and I learn that it is the result of an accident he suffered long ago in a pub. Some chaps were playing darts, and one dart missed the board and landed in Mr. Simmons' eye.

Mrs. Simmons has dark piercing eyes that are slightly crossed and black hair that is pulled tightly back to the base of her neck and gathered into a bun. She reminds me of the witches in the Grimm fairy tales. The Simmonses have two sons, Joey, who is twelve, and Kenny, who is about Ephraim's age. After inspecting me up and down, the boys find me uninteresting and ignore me, which suits me very well because I feel awkward with them. Mrs. Simmons shows me where I am to sleep, a small room at the far end of the second level that is used for storage. They call it the "box room." The box room has no windows and has a strange, musty smell. She tells me in her strangled Yiddish that she would like me to call them Aunty and Uncle. To make sure I understand, she digs her finger into her impressive bosom and says, "*Ich* Aunty." Mrs. Simmons buys me new underwear, a jumper, and a pair of shiny black Wellingtons. And one pair of "half-shoes" with laces, also black.

The Simmonses are not strictly Orthodox, although they keep a kosher home. On Shabbos morning Mr. Simmons takes me and the boys to shul. The streets are covered in slush and ice and so I wear my new Wellingtons. The shul is much larger and quite different from Papa's little *shtiebel.* There is a women's section upstairs, but Mr. Simmons lets me sit next to him in the men's section. The old men make a big fuss over me and, in between taking pinches of snuff, they take pinches out of my plump cheeks, which seem to be irresistible to old men. Even the rabbi has to take a pinch; except I find it hard to believe he's the rabbi because, besides being a short little man with a large paunch, he's completely *clean shaven*. How can a rabbi not wear a beard? "Perhaps," I think to myself, "in England it's allowed." But the rabbi is very friendly to me and when taking his pinch out of my cheek he smiles and says in Yiddish, "Welcome to London, little girl." By the time the *davening* is over, my cheeks are aching.

After the service there is a hasty *Kiddush* at the shul, where they serve herring, which I don't like, and an even hastier lunch at home consisting of cheese sandwiches, which I also don't like, but I'm too afraid of Mrs. Simmons to tell her that, so I say I'm not hungry. Then Mrs. Simmons announces that we are going on an outing in the afternoon, to something called "the flicks" for which we mustn't be late. We take a bus to the Astoria Cinema to see a picture starring a little girl called Shirley Temple. This is the first time I have ever been to a cinema and I am so excited that for a while I forget the guilt that is nibbling at my insides because I am, for the first time in my life, desecrating Shabbos. I sit open-mouthed, looking around at the dark blue velvet walls and up at the ceiling, which is covered with twinkling stars to create the illusion that we're under an open night sky. There are balconies and balustrades up and down the walls from which hang exotic tapestries and rugs. Life-sized figures of Spanish señoritas and sombrero-hatted señores dressed in their native costumes loll around in different poses. There is a man playing an organ, which rises up from the pit beneath the stage like an oyster coming out of its shell. Pretty female usherettes in smart uniforms strut up and down the aisles. Suspended from their necks are trays containing cigarettes and a mouth-watering assortment of sweets and chocolates. The organ and the organist slowly disappear into the pit, the curtain rises, and the picture begins. Shirley Temple is enchanting with her curly mop and dimples, especially when she sings and dances, and for the first few minutes I am mesmerized by the performance on the screen even though I don't understand one word that is spoken or what the film is about. The padded seats are so comfortable and I am so sleepy....

I'm jolted awake by a blow to the side of my head. The picture is over and we all stand at attention as the screen is filled with a photograph of King George the Sixth in a naval uniform plastered with medals, sitting on a white horse and saluting. The organist plays "God Save the King." Mrs. Simmons is barely able to contain her fury and glares at me angrily the whole time the anthem is playing. Then she drags me outside by the arm, her face flushed with rage. I can't understand why she is so upset. Eventually, after a lot of broken Yiddish, hand signals and much yelling, it becomes clear that I have wasted the Simmonses' money by falling asleep in the cinema. Going to the flicks is a special treat, and I am an ungrateful little girl who doesn't deserve such special treats. My head is throbbing, but I am determined not to cry. Throughout Mrs. Simmons' harangue Joey stands close to her wearing a smirk on his face while Kenny looks away in embarrassment. Mr. Simmons stands at a distance staring into a shop window, either pretending to be deaf or that he doesn't know us.

I can't help feeling that this is my punishment for going to the flicks on Shabbos.

In bed that night, after I recite the Shema, I beg God's forgiveness. But then I add, "But, dear God, I can't promise you it won't happen again because it's not up to me. It's up to Mrs. Simmons." I dream of Papa. He is *davening* but I can't see his face because it is hidden under his *tallis*. All I can see of him is his left arm and the black leather straps of his tefillin coiled around it. *Papa, Papa, it wasn't my fault*, I protest to him in my dream. But he ignores me. He puts his *tallis*-covered head down to rest on his left arm and continues *davening*.

And, of course, it does happen again. And again. The next time, though, it's not to a cinema that we go but to the Hippodrome in the West End to see a live pantomime and music hall show. By this time, I understand English well enough to stay wide awake throughout the performances. There are acrobats and jugglers, mimes, singers and dancers, and dogs jumping through hoops. There is even a trained bear doing tricks on a large ball. In one scene a beautiful lady sits under a tree singing a song with which I am already familiar because they play it so often on the wireless: "Underneath the Spreading Chestnut Tree." The lady is dressed in a long, pink, Empire gown with a green sash under her bust, and on her head she wears a large hat with a wide floppy brim to match. The scene is irresistibly romantic.

Mrs. Simmons enrolls me in the local County Council school, where I enter the first form. After two months, I have forgotten almost all my German and Yiddish. Without realizing it, I have begun speaking English like a native. I love school and I love my teacher, Miss Richards. She spends extra time with me to make sure I understand the lessons. Once she sees that I have learned how to read she introduces me to the books in the school library. Enid Blyton immediately becomes my favorite author and I devour her books. Miss Richards talks to Mrs. Simmons about getting me a library card so that I can borrow books from the Whitechapel library.

Miss Richards says it's important to know how many days there are in each month and she teaches us a special song to help us remember:

Thirty days has September,
April, June, and November.
All the rest have thirty-one,
Excepting February alone,
Which has but twenty-eight days clear,
And twenty-nine in each leap year.

At first, during our playground breaks, the children are not very friendly and sometimes won't let me play with them, but Miss

Richards makes them let me join in; once they see that I know how to skip rope and throw the ball, they are happy to include me. Eventually they even fight among themselves to get me on their teams.

The only thing I don't like about school is having to walk there and back with Joey and Kenny. Kenny is all right, but Joey keeps making fun of my English and calls me a *Kraut*. I don't know what *Kraut* means, but the way he says it – and with such a mean expression on his face – I know it can't be anything nice.

Once a week, Mrs. Perlow and her daughter bring Mimi to visit me. Today Mimi walks in holding the Perlow girl's hand. A feeling I have never felt before bubbles up inside my chest and, for the first time since I have been living with the Simmonses, I feel I can't hold back my tears. Immediately Mimi drops the Perlow girl's hand, pulls me onto her lap, and admires the new "half-shoes" I am wearing. She, too, has "half-shoes" and is wearing a new jumper and skirt. Mimi says, "Friedl, your shoes are much nicer than the Ginzburg girls' shoes." And all is well again.

We are not left alone together for a moment and so I cannot tell Mimi how Mrs. Simmons, with a look of disgust on her face and pinching her nose with one hand, made a bundle of all my clothes and threw them into the rubbish together with my tattered suitcase, which still contained the yo-yo Opa Shmuel gave me. I cannot tell Mimi how upset Mrs. Simmons is that I'm unable to call her Aunty as she would like; much as I try, I cannot say the word. When I need to tell her something I run all the way down-stairs or upstairs, depending on where she is, rather than call her Aunty. I cannot tell Mimi how sometimes I have nightmares and walk in my sleep and how Mrs. Simmons screams at me when I wet my bed ("...they are not paying me enough for this," she yells) and punishes me by sending me to bed without supper. I cannot tell Mimi how, when I spilled the salt water at the Pesach Seder table Mrs. Simmons pointed her witch's finger at me and, with her black eyes piercing right through me and her voice dripping with venom, accused me of having *German blood*! Nor can I tell

Mimi how Joey corners me when Kenny is not around and his parents are both downstairs in the shop, and pushes me onto the floor, lies down on top of me, pressing down so hard that I feel I am suffocating, and just when I feel I can't take another breath, he gets off me with the warning that he'll kill me if I tell his parents what he did.

No, I am unable to tell Mimi any of these things, and so, when she asks me in front of Mrs. Perlow and Mrs. Simmons, "How are you, Friedl, are you happy?" I just nod and smile and say, "Yes, of course I'm happy."

*   *   *

The summer arrives and passes. Occasionally Mimi receives a postcard from Mama, which she reads to me during her visits. Some of the German words have become foreign to me and Mimi has to translate. Papa has fled to Yugoslavia to avoid the roundups, but Mama refuses to leave Oma, who cannot undertake such a long journey, and so the two of them have remained in Vienna. In one postcard Mama says, "I am worried about Friedl. Is she all right?" Sometimes Mimi receives a letter with a Manchester postmark from Erika. She is fine, Erika writes, even though she complains that Tante Regina is a slave driver and makes her work too hard. Tante Regina also writes sometimes and complains that Erika is lazy. Ephraim has found out where we are and writes regularly, and every few weeks he sends me a bar of chocolate, which he buys with his pocket money. He says he receives sixpence a week. Occasionally Mimi also hears from Tante Rosa. She and Onkel Benno did not stay in England long and are now in America. I wonder where America is. In my mind I imagine America and Palestine lying side by side, merely connected by an invisible border, and I wonder whether when Tante Rosa arrived in America she was able to visit cousin Mina in Palestine.

On Sundays, if the weather is fine, Mrs. Simmons packs up a picnic basket with fried chicken, potato crisps, and pickles and all of us ride on the No. 653 bus to Springfield Park near Clapton Common. There, she spreads a blanket on the grass and sends me off to play ball with the boys or gives me some bread to feed the ducks in the pond. But I don't want to play ball with Joey and Kenny. They always make me the monkey-in-the-middle and never let me have the ball. Nor am I very interested in feeding the ducks. All I want to do is go on the swings. I am proud to have learned how to "pump" and can swing for hours and hours without getting tired. When I propel myself ever higher and higher I close my eyes and imagine launching myself off the swing into the air and sailing on and on right up into the sky. Up, up into the sky and beyond....

*   *   *

September 1939. All the London schools are being evacuated. After Germany's invasion of Poland, England declared war on Germany and it is expected that London will soon be bombed. The British government announces that getting the children out of London and into the safety of the countryside is a priority. Mrs. Simmons stuffs my few clothes into a knapsack, shoves a paper bag into my hands that contains some cheese sandwiches and an apple, and takes me and Joey and Kenny to school. It is a beautiful Indian summer's day with a cool breeze coming off the River Thames to the east of us. Way up above, in the clear sky, sails a fleet of barrage balloons, swaying gently in the breeze. Mrs. Simmons says that the balloons are meant to hinder the enemy's planes.

When we arrive at school, we find the assembly hall filled with children sitting on the floor waiting for buses. Mrs. Simmons tells me to plunk myself down, then says, "Goodbye, be a good girl," and leaves with Joey and Kenny trailing after her. Someone comes around handing out small cardboard boxes containing gas masks with straps to hang around our necks. We are put through a gas mask drill to learn how to use them. I like the fresh rubber smell against my nose, and when I look through the glass in the upper part of the mask and see all the other children in their masks, I have to laugh. They all look like creatures from the planet Mars. I wonder where Mimi is. I haven't seen her this week. She goes to a different school and I wonder if she's also being evacuated. There is an announcement. We are broken up into groups. Our group of about ten children is introduced to Mr. Anderson, a teacher who will accompany us. Mr. Anderson says we are going to a little village in Surrey called Thorpe, where we'll be in his charge. I'm glad that Joey and Kenny are not in my group. Afterward I learn that Mrs. Simmons decided to take them back home. Later they are evacuated to a different part of the country.

I never see the Simmonses again.

CHAPTER THREE

THORPE

Once again I'm on a train, but this time the compartment is comfortable and warm, and instead of traveling over a snow-covered terrain, the train rumbles over lush green fields and meadows and gurgling brooks and streams. I make friends with a girl my age, Millie, a Cockney from Stepney, whose English is hard for me to understand. Millie drops and adds "aitches" in an alarming manner that is not at all like Miss Richards' English. She hauls out a piece of dirty string from her pocket and we amuse ourselves by playing Cat's Cradle until, about one hour into the journey, the train pulls to a screeching halt into the station called Thorpe. "Cor blimey," says Millie. "'Ere we are. We've harrived, 'aven't we!"

When we alight from the train we hear loud music coming from one end of the platform where a straggly three-piece brass band is welcoming us with "Pack Up Your Troubles in Your Old Kit Bag and Smile, Smile, Smile." At the other end of the platform a small group of people is waiting. These are the villagers of Thorpe; they have come to select the children who will live with them for the duration of the war. Mr. Anderson shepherds us toward the crowd. They look very friendly and everyone smiles encouragingly at us. Two of the women point to me and whisper to Mr. Anderson who whispers back. I overhear the words *Jewish* and *refugee*, and their eyes wander away from me. One by one the children are chosen and leave with their new "parents," until finally Mr. Anderson and I are the only ones left on the platform.

Suddenly a tall, slim lady with dark bobbed hair, dressed in a tweed skirt and light blue twin set, comes bounding up the stairs to the platform accompanied by a beautiful golden dog on a leash. I fall in love with both of them on sight. "Please, God," I pray silently, "please." The lady has the lively, vivacious air and sparkling blue eyes that the lady in the music hall show had, the one who sang "Underneath the Spreading Chestnut Tree." The lady goes up to Mr. Anderson. "I do hope I'm not too late," she gasps, quite out of breath. Then she crouches down in front of me until we are both at eye level. "I'm Mrs. Whyte-Smith," she says, "and this is my dog, Rusty Rufus Reginald Roo, but we call him Rusty, for short. You may pet him, if you like." Which I do, and Rusty reacts by wagging his tail wildly and slobbering all over my face. "Rusty obviously likes you," says Mrs. Whyte-Smith, "and any friend of Rusty's is a friend of mine."

God has answered my prayers.

* * *

Dear Friedl,

I am sending this letter to you care of Mrs. Simmons and I hope you get it, wherever you are. Mrs. Perlow told me that you were evacuated. As you can see, I was also evacuated. Everything happened so fast I didn't have a chance to get in touch with you beforehand. I'm staying in a little village in Yorkshire. The nearest town is Leeds. It took a few hours to get here by train. The *goyim* I am staying with are very nice except that Mr. Evans is a farmer and he raises pigs, which are the most disgusting animals! I received a letter from America, from Tante Rosa. She said that because this is an emergency we have to eat whatever we are given, even *chazer treif.* I'm not sure she's right, especially as she's not at all religious herself, but I don't want to upset Mr. and Mrs. Evans by refusing anything. They have one son who is in the navy, on a submarine.

I received a postcard from Mama which was forwarded to me by Mrs. Perlow. The Germans sent Oma to a town in Czechoslovakia called Theresienstadt, which is a special place for old people. Mama is now in Yugoslavia together with Papa. Oma Blima is also with them. They are waiting for a ship to take them to Palestine.

I hope the *goyim* where you are living are nice. Please let me know how you are getting on.

Love and kisses,
Your sister Mimi

* * *

Dear Mimi,

I got your letter. It made me happy. My *goyim* are called Colonel and Mrs. Whyte-Smith. Their house is called Morley Manor. They don't have any children, but they have a beautiful Irish setter dog with long floppy ears. His name is Rusty. That's his nickname, not his full name. The house is very big. There are two staircases, one in the front and one in the back. The back staircase is for servants. They have one maid called Annie. Annie is pretty and very nice. She wears a black uniform with a little white apron and a white cap that looks like a crown.

Annie gives me a bath *twice* a week in a real bath with hot water that comes straight out of the tap. Annie told me if water wasn't rationed I would have baths even more often. I have a big room all to myself. The bed is huge and has a pink cover like a roof over it. Annie says it is called a canopy. From my window I can see all the way to the end of the garden, where there are walnut trees. Outside my window is a big apple tree. Mrs. Whyte-Smith says that seven different kinds of apples grow on it! Sometimes Rusty sleeps on the floor near my bed. I have to use the back staircase. During the week I eat in the kitchen with Annie.

On Sundays I eat in the dining room with Colonel and Mrs. Whyte-Smith. We always eat the same thing. Hot roast mutton and Yorkshire pudding and peas, with custard for afters. I don't like custard but Mrs. Whyte-Smith doesn't mind if I leave it. She gives me a biscuit or an apple instead. On Monday we eat the leftover cold roast mutton with hot baked potatoes in their skins.

I have to go to bed now. I'll try and write more tomorrow.
Love from your sister,
Friedl

* * *

Dear Mimi:

Mrs. Whyte-Smith has been teaching me table manners. She says it's very important to have good table manners. There are special plates for bread. In between bites it's important to put one's bread on the special plate. One must also place one's hands in one's lap while one chews. It is also important to always chew with one's mouth closed. Mrs. Whyte-Smith says the bread won't run away and we don't want to catch any flies. When one is finished, one has to put the knife and fork together in the middle of the dinner plate "like two soldiers at attention." I'm allowed to eat with a knife but I have to hold it in my right hand with the fork in my left hand. It's not easy to keep the peas on the back of the fork. They keep falling off. But Mrs. Whyte-Smith says it's not good manners to pile them up on the front of the fork. Every day after school, Annie helps me to practice my table manners.

I've got to go now because Mrs. Whyte-Smith wants to take me and Rusty for a walk in the woods.

Love and kisses,

Your sister, Frieda (Mrs. Whyte-Smith says Friedl sounds too German.)

P.S. I haven't wet my bed once since I got here.

*　*　*

Dear Frieda,

Your *goyim* sound very nice. The Evanses have dogs too, but I'm a bit afraid of them. One of them is a big bulldog and he growls and barks a lot, though Mr. Evans says his bark is worse than his bite. But I don't want to find out. I am learning to milk cows. Mrs. Evans wakes me very early in the morning when it's still dark outside, about five o'clock, which I really don't like at all. But I'm getting quite good at milking. I also like collecting eggs from the chicken coop. At least I don't have to work in the pigsty. Soon I will be starting school and then I won't have to get up so early to milk. There is a special school for the evacuated children but it's not starting until next week. Are you going to school? There are some other Jewish children here but I'm the only one from Vienna.

Ephraim wrote that he is trying to get the people in charge of his hostel to let me and you live there also, but so far they only want boys.

Please write often and let me know how you're getting on.
Love and kisses,
Mimi

*   *   *

Dear Mimi:

I like the school here. The school is called St. Mary's. There's a special room for the evacuated children. Mr. Anderson is our teacher. He came with us from London. Mr. Anderson's wife died last year of a bad illness. He has no children. I am very sorry for him. He's even older than Papa and has almost no hair, but he's very nice to me. I am the only Jew. I am also the only refugee. There is one girl my age, Millie, who comes from Stepney. There are three older girls and the rest are boys. Some of the boys are very mean. The other day two of them followed me home from school and called me horrible names. They sang "Roll out the barrel, we've got the Jews on the run." Then one of them got hold of me and the other one tried to take down my knickers. They said they wanted to see if Jewish girls are made the same way as Christian girls. I kicked so hard that one of the boys got a bloody nose and the other one let go of me. I managed to run away. When I told Mrs. Whyte-Smith, she was very angry. She said she will speak to Mr. Anderson.

Please write soon.

Love, Frieda

*   *   *

Throw Your Feet Over Your Shoulders

Dear Mimi:

As you can see, I am learning to write properly, like grown-ups do. I hope you can read my handwriting. Mr. Anderson has lent me a lot of books. I love *The Wind in the Willows* and *Little Lord Fauntleroy*. He also told me about a magazine for girls called *The Girls' Crystal*. It comes out every Tuesday. When I told Mrs. Whyte-Smith about it she bought it for me. There are some very good stories in there. Some of them are stories that go on every week. I think they're called serials. The one I like best is about two boys and two girls who have adventures in America in a place called Arizona. There is a huge desert in Arizona and a lot of cactus plants. Do they have that magazine where you live? You should try and get it.

Love and kisses,
Your sister Frieda

*   *   *

Dear Mimi:

Mrs. Whyte-Smith is teaching me how to darn socks. There is a wooden thing that looks like a huge mushroom. One puts it into the sock so that the hole shows. Then one darns the hole in the same color wool as the sock. If I don't darn the hole tight enough Mrs. Whyte-Smith cuts the hole even larger. Then I have to start all over again. So I try to get it right the first time. She is also teaching me how to knit. Every Monday night some women come to knit in Mrs. Whyte-Smith's drawing room. They are knitting socks and hats for the soldiers. I don't know how to knit socks. You need three needles for socks. So I'm knitting a scarf in khaki wool.

Annie says it's time for my bath.

Love from your sister Frieda

*   *   *

Dear Mimi:

The other day when I was in the W.C. I overheard the older girls talking. They were talking about something awful that happens to girls once a month. They called it a "curse." It sounded really disgusting. But then I realized that those girls are not Jewish so this must be something that only happens to *shiksas*. Do you know anything about this?

The Colonel is a lot older than Mrs. Whyte-Smith. He was a colonel in another war called the Great War. He told me that he fought in France. When he said that, I remembered some of the French words Mama taught us, *Quelleheurestil, Jenesaispas, Commentallezvous.* I tried them out on the Colonel, but he didn't understand me. Or perhaps he didn't hear because he's a bit deaf. One has to shout at him a lot. He keeps holding this big horn called an ear trumpet to his ear and saying, "Eh what, eh what?" over and over again. The ear trumpet reminds me of the *shofar* Papa used to blow on Rosh Hashanah. The Colonel has a white moustache and smokes a pipe. He wears tweed trousers called "plus fours" and he carries a thick walking stick wherever he goes.

Love and kisses from your sister Frieda

*   *   *

Dear Mimi:

Did I mention that the Colonel is the head of the village Home Guard? Every morning he and a lot of other old soldiers meet on the Common with their rifles. Then they march off into St. Anne's Woods for what they call "war maneuvers." The Colonel told me the Home Guard will protect us if the Germans attack. So we have nothing to worry about. In the downstairs lavatory all the rifles hang on the wall opposite the toilet. There is a name printed above each rifle. I'm a bit frightened to go to the lavatory with all those rifles, and so I try to use the upstairs lavatory whenever I can.

One of the other downstairs rooms is the Colonel's "war room." I'm only allowed in there if he invites me. The other day he invited me and showed me all the maps on the walls. The maps have little colored pins all over them. The Colonel explained that the pins show the progress of the battles and different "fronts" of the war. The blue pins are for the Allies and the red pins are for the Germans. There are a lot more red pins than blue pins. Except when he's busy with the Home Guard, the Colonel spends most of the day in his war room.

Please write soon.

Love and kisses, your sister Frieda

*   *   *

Dear Mimi:

I got your last letter. I hope your cold is better.

Mrs. Whyte-Smith drives a little car called an Austin. She doesn't use the car much because petrol is rationed. But last Sunday she took me in the car to Chertsey, which is about an hour away. We had tea in Ye Olde Tea Shoppe on High Street. While we were sitting having our tea an old friend of Mrs. Whyte-Smith's came in. Mrs. Whyte-Smith said, "What a coincidence!" He was in a strange uniform and Mrs. Whyte-Smith said he is a Yank, an American soldier, what they call a "G.I." His name is Andy and he's very handsome and friendly and sat with us for quite a long time. He gave me some chewing gum. He held Mrs. Whyte-Smith's hand and whispered into her ear. And she laughed a lot and whispered back. I couldn't hear what they said. On the way home, Mrs. Whyte-Smith asked me not to tell the Colonel that we met her old friend Andy in Chertsey. She said the Colonel doesn't like Americans. So I won't.

Please write again soon.

Love and kisses,

Yours sister, Frieda

* * *

Dear Friedl:

Finally, Mimi sent me your address so I'm sending you a Kit-Kat bar which I bought with my pocket money. I am very upset that you and Mimi are living with *goyim*. Did you remember that it was Rosh Hashanah on September 14th and Yom Kippur on the 23rd? After Yom Kippur came Sukkos. Do you remember the *sukkah* we had behind Papa's *shtiebel* and how we decorated it with bunches of artificial grapes and apples and colored paper chains? How we sat in there with our overcoats and gloves on because it was so cold and how Mama and Oma came down with the food and kept it warm by wrapping blankets around the saucepans? Are there any other Jews in Thorpe besides you? Does everyone know you are Jewish? Do you hear from Mr. and Mrs. Simmons? I wish you and Mimi could be with me here in Cardiff where everyone in the hostel is Jewish. Chanukah is early this year, December 7th, before any of our birthdays. Is there anyone in Thorpe who can light a Chanukah menorah? I hope you will write to me very soon.

Love from your brother,

Ephraim

P.S. Are you remembering to say the Shema every night before you go to sleep?

* * *

Thorpe is an idyllic, sleepy little English village in the county of Surrey in the district of Runnymede where the Magna Carta was signed by King John in the year 1215. It is only about thirty miles from the center of London. It has many country lanes lined with many quaint little cottages with thatched roofs, mullioned windows, white picket fences, and a colorful profusion of flowers. The village has one of everything. Or almost one of everything. One sweets shop, one tobacconist-cum-post office, one butcher, one baker, one grocer, one school called St. Mary's, and one church, also called St. Mary's, which dates back to the twelfth century. And naturally there is one pub, The Windsor Arms, probably so named because Thorpe lies practically in the shadow of Windsor Castle, just a few miles away. There is one main thoroughfare, High Street, which cuts right through the village, and of course a village green, the Common, where the school's sports events take place and where the villagers stroll and sit and gossip when the weather is fine, and where children of all ages fly their kites. Or, rather, where they used to fly their kites before the war. Kite-flying has been prohibited "for the duration"; the government fears that some of the higher-flying kites might interfere with planes or barrage balloons, or might even be mistaken for enemy planes and draw unnecessary fire from our antiaircraft guns.

Thorpe has an apology of a river, the River Bourne, which is not much more than a ditch and runs alongside the main road. Eventually it joins up with the Thames somewhere. Flanking the village are St. Anne's Woods, Rusty's favorite destination for our walks and one of mine too. Mrs. Whyte-Smith has taught me to recognize some of the flora in the woods, and I especially love to pick the bluebells that grow there in abundance. Whatever cannot be had in Thorpe can be found in Staines, just a few minutes away by car or bus.

When air-raid sirens go off in London, they usually sound in Thorpe as well, and then Mrs. Whyte-Smith immediately calls us together and we run down to the Anderson shelter at the end of the garden beneath the walnut trees. The shelter has been dug several feet into the ground and the roof is made of corrugated tin. It is barely large enough for the four of us. In it there is a bench, some pillows and blankets, a supply of water and biscuits, and some torches, candles, and matches. At night, because of the blackout, we are not allowed to turn on the torches or light the candles until the door has been securely fastened. Sometimes we have to spend the whole night down there before the all-clear sounds; we don't get much sleep then, and by morning the air in the shelter is stale and sticky. Apart from the fact that there is not enough room for anyone to lie down, it's impossible to sleep anyway because of the constant pounding and thudding of the bombs raining down on London. At times a stray bomb makes us flinch when it comes down a bit too close for comfort; the earth shakes around us and Annie says, "Whew, that was a close one," and when we climb out of the shelter we are relieved to find the house still standing. Sometimes the horizon is red and smoky from the fires still smoldering in London. (Is that Anderson shelter responsible for my fear of enclosed places? Even when going to the theater or movies I tend to become anxious if I don't have an aisle seat, as if needing a ready escape route. This holds true even when I attend synagogue. Does this signify a lack of faith on my part?)

When the siren sounds in the middle of the night, Mrs. Whyte-Smith has to wake me. I am such a sound sleeper that not only don't I hear the siren, but very often I fall out of bed in my sleep and continue sleeping on the floor without waking up. If the siren sounds during school hours, all the children, the local Thorpe children and the London evacuees, run down to a basement room in the main building of the school that has been converted into a bomb shelter. Sometimes we continue having lessons in the shelter until the all-clear sounds. Several times during the term we have air-raid drills to practice running down to the shelter in an orderly fashion.

Every day after school Annie and I have high tea in the

kitchen. Many items of food are rationed, but bread and margarine are plentiful so we eat a lot of it. Margarine sandwiches with strawberry jam; margarine sandwiches with watercress; margarine sandwiches with cucumbers; margarine sandwiches with Marmite. Annie also makes delicious scones. While we eat we listen to the *Children's Hour* on the wireless. Annie loves the *Children's Hour* just as much as I do. There are wonderful stories read or acted out by real actors, sometimes child actors and sometimes grown-up actors like Greer Garson and Walter Pidgeon. Some of the stories are serialized so there is something to look forward to every day when I come home from school.

Every now and then, Princess Elizabeth and her younger sister, Princess Margaret, are on the *Children's Hour*. Sometimes Princess Elizabeth reads a poem. At the end of the hour she always says the same thing: "Good night children, everywhere." Then she prompts her sister, "Say good night, Margaret." And six-year-old Margaret obediently says, "Good night children." Annie tells me that the princesses were really not supposed to be princesses; they only became princesses because their Uncle David didn't want to be king and handed the throne over to his brother, the princesses' father, who is now King George the Sixth.

"Poor little buggers," Annie says, and when I ask her why, she says something that really puzzles me.

"I wouldn't want to be in those poor girls' shoes," Annie says, "for all the tea in China."

Sometimes, while we are listening to the *Children's Hour*, we are interrupted by either the Colonel or Mrs. Whyte-Smith ringing for Annie. When this happens, Annie looks up at the row of bells above the kitchen door to see which one of them is summoning her. "Bloody hell," she says, "they can bloody well wait." If it's the Colonel calling for her, he gets very impatient and keeps ringing and ringing until Annie finally throws down her dish towel in disgust and goes to see what he wants.

"Just remember, ducky," she says to me before she flounces

through the door, "patience is a virtue; possess it if you can. Seldom found in woman, but *never* in a man!"

* * *

My seventh birthday falls on Monday, December 18th, a week before Christmas. Erika and Miriam and Ephraim each send me a card; Ephraim also sends a Kit-Kat bar. Mrs. Whyte-Smith gives me a porcelain doll for my birthday, a boy doll whom I name Peter. Peter comes with a Boy Scout uniform. I've never had a doll before and I'm not sure what to do with him. "Take him into the bath with you, ducky," Annie says, "and give him a good scrub," which I do, but I think perhaps I'm a little too old for dolls.

I had been hoping for a bicycle, but I don't tell Annie that. The people Millie's staying with, who own the sweets shop, have let Millie use an old bike that belonged to their daughter who's married and moved away. Millie and I both learned to ride on it. I've decided I love bicycling even more than I love pumping on the swings. Every night, after I've said the Shema, I pray that when I wake up in the morning there will be a bicycle standing outside my bedroom door. But so far my prayers haven't been answered. Mrs. Whyte-Smith says, "What rotten luck, having your birthday just a week before Christmas." She says she would have made more of a fuss of my birthday if she hadn't been so busy preparing for the holidays and that she will make it up to me then. I can't help wondering if God will answer my prayers at Christmas and send me a bike, but then I remember that Christmas is a *goyish* holiday so perhaps God won't recognize it as a real holiday.

I haven't answered Ephraim's last letter, nor Mimi's, because I don't know what to say. I know they'll be upset if I mention Christmas and how I'm going to be an angel in a play called "A Pilgrim's Progress," which will be performed in St. Mary's Church hall. My scene takes place in the manger with little baby Jesus lying in his crèche surrounded by the three wise men. Above all, I can't tell them that Annie has been taking me to church every

Sunday and that I've even followed her example and knelt to the Jesus hanging on the cross above the altar. Nor that I've been attending Sunday school where I'm learning all about the *goyish* saints. I am particularly fascinated with the story of St. Joan of Arc. Annie says that on a clear night, if you look up into the sky, you can see the saints sitting on their thrones. I keep staring and staring up into the night sky until my neck is stiff, but so far I haven't spotted any saints. I enjoy singing the hymns in church, especially "Rock of Ages." Annie says there's no harm in my saying the Lord's Prayer at night right after I say Shema, now that I know it by heart, and so I do. "Our Father, who art in heaven, hallowed be Thy name...."

So I decide I won't write to Ephraim and Mimi until after Christmas. Instead I send them each a birthday card that I made myself. All three of us have our birthdays in December. Their birthdays are on the ninth and tenth. At home in Vienna we used to receive a bar of chocolate on our birthdays, and Oma Blima would send over her famous chocolate-coconut balls. On the night before my birthday, I dream of Oma Perl. I dream that she is grating chocolate, endlessly grating and grating and grating into several huge bowls that are filling up quickly and overflowing with chocolate shavings. Oma is unable to keep up with the speed at which the bowls are filling up. *Why are you grating so much chocolate, Oma?* I ask her in my dream. *For your birthday, you silly goose,* she says. *Did you think I would forget your birthday?*

Sometimes, Mr. Anderson brings a sack of potatoes to our classroom and we roast them on the black iron stove that stands in the middle of the room, and eat them while they are piping hot and crusty. The day before we break up for the Christmas holidays, he brings in a big bag of chestnuts and we have a lot of fun roasting them and watching them pop and crack open and jump all over the place on top of the stove. There is a lot of laughing and giggling when the chestnuts pop open and we try to catch them and drop them quickly because they burn our fingers. We put our scalded fingers into our mouths or shake our hands in the air screaming, "Ooh, ooh, ouch!" All of us except the bully boys love Mr. Anderson. We have chipped in our few pennies' pocket money to buy Mr. Anderson a tie for Christmas. Mrs. Whyte-Smith went to Staines especially to buy it. It has what she calls "regimental stripes," and Mr. Anderson says he loves it and will wear it when he goes to London to spend Christmas with his elderly parents.

For the few days before Christmas, Mrs. Whyte-Smith and Annie bustle around the kitchen making all sorts of biscuits, pies, cakes, and mincemeats, letting me help now and then with the mixing. They let me lick out the bowls after each mixture is in the oven. Most important of all, they prepare the Christmas pudding. On top of one of the kitchen cupboards there are two big earthenware bowls covered with cloth and tied tightly with string around the rim. These contain Christmas puddings, which are labeled with the dates of two previous years. This Christmas we'll eat the pudding labeled 1937. The pudding Annie and Mrs. Whyte-Smith prepare now will be labeled 1939 and is meant to be eaten on Christmas Day 1941. Annie tells me they put a lot of rum into the puddings to preserve them and also some pennies, ha'pennies, and farthings.

"So mind your teeth when you eat it, ducky," she warns me, "and be careful not to swallow the coins."

The one who finds the most money is supposed to have good luck for the whole year.

I help Mrs. Whyte-Smith and Annie decorate the huge Christmas tree that stands in the corner of the drawing room and reaches almost to the ceiling. Mrs. Whyte-Smith doesn't let the Colonel help because she says he just gets in the way, and besides, he is too busy running the war. There are all sorts of colored balls and streamers and ornaments, which we hang from the branches. When we are almost finished, Annie holds the ladder and I climb up and fasten a white sparkling angel all the way at the top. After that, Mrs. Whyte-Smith and Annie thread colored lights through the branches. Then they turn off the overhead lights and turn on the colored lights, and the sight of the tree so beautifully decorated and lit up makes us all gasp.

On Christmas Eve all the wrapped presents are placed around the foot of the tree to be opened the following day. Outside some singers from the church choir go from door to door singing "Silent Night" and "Good King Wenceslas" and other carols. There is a sprinkling of snow on the ground and the whole scene looks just like a Christmas card except, of course, that everyone's house is blacked out and there are no streetlights burning so it's a bit eerie. When I go to bed that night, Mrs. Whyte-Smith hangs a long stocking made of a kind of netting at the foot of my bed. She tells me Father Christmas will come during the night and fill it with presents. I try to stay awake but the next thing I know, it's morning. I spring out of bed, but before examining the stocking I open the door to see if my bicycle is leaning against the wall. The hallway is empty. I'm bitterly disappointed but I silently assure God that it's all right; I don't blame Him.

The Christmas stocking is bulging with all sorts of tantalizing items. There are little notebooks, some crayons, a bar of Cadbury's milk chocolate, and a torch with extra batteries. There is also a plain wooden yo-yo. I'm especially happy with the torch because now I will be able to read under the covers after Annie says "Lights out." I notice that there is still something stuck in the toe of the stocking, and I put in my hand and pull out a little book. *A Child's Garden of Verses* by Robert Louis Stevenson. As soon as I open it, I forget about my disappointment over the bicycle. The minute I read "I have a little shadow that goes in and out with me/And what can be the use of him is more than I can see...," I'm hooked. I become so engrossed that Annie has to call me several times to come down for breakfast before I hear her.

Later there is a lavish dinner of stuffed turkey and mashed potatoes and gravy and peas (which I've almost mastered), followed, of course, by the 1937 Christmas pudding. I find the most coins, about tuppence altogether. After dinner I'm very sleepy, and the Colonel says it's because of the rum in the pudding. But I manage to stay awake for the opening of the presents. We all go into the drawing room where a roaring coal fire is burning in the grate and the Christmas tree is twinkling above the presents scattered beneath its branches. Mrs. Whyte-Smith gives me a beautiful green cardigan that she knitted especially for me. It has intricate cables down the front and on the sleeves, and will go well with the skirts and brogues and kneesocks Mrs. Whyte-Smith bought for me soon after I arrived in Thorpe.

When I try on the cardigan Mrs. Whyte-Smith says, "Now you look like a proper English schoolgirl, especially with your blond plaits. No one would guess that you're a Jewish refugee."

I receive more books and a game of Tiddlywinks, and also a beautiful red leather-bound diary with a lock and key. Best of all, the Colonel gives me a Brownie camera with a roll of film. He says, "Now you can send a photo of yourself to your parents so they can see we are taking good care of you." I give the Colonel and Mrs. Whyte-Smith a painting I did in school of Rusty standing in front of Morley Manor for which Mr. Anderson made a little wooden frame. It's not a very good likeness of Rusty, but I think I did a fairly good job on the house, especially the brick chimney and the Tudor beams. Mrs. Whyte-Smith makes a big fuss over it and immediately hangs it on the scullery wall. To Annie I give a box of embroidered handkerchiefs, which I bought with my own money, and a Christmas card I made myself. Did I mention that Mrs. Whyte-Smith gives me thrupence a week pocket money? That doesn't include *The Girls' Crystal* she buys for me every week, which also costs thrupence.

*   *   *

The Simmonses have been bombed out of their flat and shop. I get the news from Mimi who heard it from the Perlows. The whole building was destroyed. Luckily they were taking shelter in the Whitechapel underground station at the time, and nobody was hurt. Because Whitechapel is so close to the East India Docks and shipyards, which are a prime target for the German bombers, it's not surprising that the Simmonses' building was hit. As my official foster parents, I suppose they are still getting an allowance for me from the government, but except for an occasional postcard asking how I'm getting on, I don't hear from them, and I rarely write back. In the past, they have once or twice mentioned that they plan to visit me, but so far they haven't turned up.

In school we have been making huge cardboard signs with large block letters in lots of different colors, saying "DIG FOR VICTORY" and "LOOSE LIPS SINK SHIPS" and "WASTE NOT, WANT NOT." We have a lot of fun going around the village with Mr. Anderson, hanging the signs on trees and inside and outside the shops. He makes a point of hanging the "LOOSE LIPS SINK SHIPS" sign in the Windsor Arms, though Mr. Anderson says, "A lot of good that'll do once they're all blotto."

We know spring has arrived when we spot little yellow daffodils and crocuses pushing up through the thawing earth. When the weather gets a bit warmer, Mrs. Whyte-Smith tells me that the whole garden at the back of Morley Manor has to be converted into a victory garden. The three of us, Mrs. Whyte-Smith, Annie, and I, armed with shovels and hoes, dig up most of the bushes, even the rosebushes. The only ones we leave are the gooseberry and red- and black-currant bushes and one raspberry bush. After we've thoroughly turned, hoed, weeded, and treated the soil with mulch, we plant seeds of potatoes, string beans, peas, cabbages, cucumbers, carrots, and tomatoes, and then we saturate the whole area with water. At the end of each row, on a little stick, we attach the empty seed packet with a picture of the vegetable in that row so we'll be able to identify it when it starts growing.

Mrs. Whyte-Smith says that I may have the small patch at the side of the house beneath the plum tree as my own little victory garden. Annie helps me make the rows straight by attaching string to little wooden pegs hammered into the soil, and I plant my own carrots, cucumbers, and radishes. Annie teaches me how to forecast the weather. After we've finished seeding, she looks up and examines the sky, and says, "Red sky at night, shepherd's delight; red sky in morning, shepherd's warning." Then she announces, "It looks like it'll be a fine day tomorrow, ducky."

Every day after I come home from school, I immediately go to my little victory plot with a watering can and water the seeds I've planted. It's a very exciting moment for me when the first shoots crop up. I run into the house and tell Mrs. Whyte-Smith and Annie, and they both come out to look and congratulate me. Every few days I make sure to weed my plot, and after a few weeks I'm able to dig up some carrots and cucumbers and actually eat the vegetables I've grown! And never have I tasted such deliciously sweet carrots.

It is a perfect summer's day and I'm working in my vegetable plot. The sun is shining brightly in a cloudless blue sky and two playful butterflies chase each other under the plum tree. A solitary, puzzled bee wanders in bewilderment through the balmy air searching for the familiar rosebushes that are no longer there. It's hard to imagine that there's a war going on with people killing each other. I can't help wondering what Mama and Papa and Oma are doing at this moment and what they would say if they could see me now, growing vegetables in my own little garden. Suddenly, an airplane, seemingly coming out of nowhere, swoops down very low, skimming the treetops. I look up and even before I see the swastikas on the wings I hear *ack-ack-ack-ack-ack*. Instinctively I know what the sound is even though I've never heard it before. Fortunately I'm at the side of the house, hidden from view by the wall and the plum tree. I shake with fright as the machine gun peppers the ground near me with bullets. The airplane zooms off into the sky.

Annie comes running out of the house calling my name.

When she sees that I'm all right, she takes my hand and races me into the house. "Lordy, that gave me quite a fright, ducky," she says. "Me, too," I say. The air-raid siren sounds, and Annie and I run outside again and down to the bottom of the garden and into the shelter just as the Colonel comes doddering out of the house led by Mrs. Whyte-Smith. Mrs. Whyte-Smith always has to tell the Colonel when it's time to go into the shelter because he can't hear the siren. A few moments later we hear a tremendous crash in the distance and the all-clear sounds. When we climb out of the shelter we see on the horizon a plume of black smoke rising into the sky. Later, on the BBC news, they announce that a stray German Messerschmidt that had been strafing the villages in our area was shot down by antiaircraft guns. Luckily nobody on the ground was hurt.

*   *   *

At the end of March I receive a letter from Ephraim together with a box of matzos and a Haggadah. He writes that Pesach begins on April fourth. I look through the Haggadah and become very sad when I realize I'm unable to read the Hebrew. I no longer even recognize the letters. What little Hebrew I was able to read and understand when I left Vienna disappeared at the same time as my Yiddish and German. I still know the Shema by heart because I've been saying it in bed every night, but I wouldn't know how to read it from a prayer book. I give Annie the box of matzos to keep in the kitchen and tell her that for a whole week starting on April fourth I will not be eating any bread. Annie is very respectful and even packs up matzah sandwiches for me to take to school. Some of the children make fun of me and the bully boys ask, "How many Christian children were killed to get enough blood to make those matzos?" I don't know what they're talking about, but luckily Mr. Anderson overhears them and punishes them with a caning across their knuckles. Of course, this doesn't make me any more popular with the bully boys. Mr. Anderson instructs Millie to walk home with me and to pick me up in the morning so I won't have to walk to and from school alone.

Sometimes Mrs. Whyte-Smith comes with Rusty to pick me up from school. Even though Rusty would probably not bite anybody, just the sight of him is enough to keep the boys at a healthy distance. Mr. Anderson tells Mrs. Whyte-Smith that he's arranging for the boys to be transferred to another village, if possible. There have been complaints about them from the homes in which they're billeted; they've been accused of vandalism and stealing from their hosts. Mr. Anderson says if he can't find other homes for them he'll have to ask their parents in London to come and take them home.

*   *   *

May 1, 1940

Dear Diary:

Last night, for the first time since I arrived at Morley Manor, I needed a night-light to fall asleep. What was even worse, I wet my bed, also for the first time. In the morning I didn't say anything to Annie. I was hoping that the sheets would dry out on their own and she wouldn't notice. But no such luck. To my surprise, Annie didn't say a word, just took off the sheets and put clean ones on the bed.

I think it happened because Annie took me to Staines to see a flick called *The Thief of Baghdad*. In it there was a genie who kept appearing in a poof of smoke. He had one blue eye and one brown eye. I was so petrified of that genie that I started to cry and Annie had to take me out of the cinema in the middle of the picture. Annie said this is just a phase and will pass. She told me to think of St. Joan and what a brave girl she was and then I won't be afraid anymore.

*   *   *

May 12, 1940
Dear Diary:

I have to tell you a secret that I've told nobody else. I can't stand the sight or taste of bacon. Even the smell of it makes me gag. Sometimes, I'm almost ready to tell Annie that I'd like porridge for breakfast or French toast, but I don't want to hurt her feelings or make extra work for her. I know Tante Rosa said we should eat everything, even *chazer treif*, but there's something about bacon that makes me feel really sick. When Annie isn't looking I slip the rashers off my plate and give them to Rusty. Rusty is always under the kitchen table waiting for scraps of food. Rusty loves bacon. Perhaps one of these days I'll tell Annie that she can have my bacon ration because I know how much she likes it.

*   *   *

At the end of July school breaks up for the six-week summer holiday. Mrs. Whyte-Smith says that because of the war nobody is going away. She says all the seaside hotels are closed and the beaches are covered with barbed wire so that even if the Germans manage to land it will not be so easy for them to advance inland. She says she and the Colonel always used to go on holiday in France or Italy; one year they even went to Austria and stayed in Vienna for a few days. The Colonel is still busy with his war exercises and his war room. Last month he was very upset with all the war news, especially about a place in France called Dunkirk. He said everyone in England who had a boat, even a rowboat, sent it over the Channel to Dunkirk to pick up British soldiers from the beach there. He was especially upset because he didn't have a boat to send. I couldn't understand what all those soldiers were doing on the beach in France, but for days the Colonel couldn't talk about anything else.

Now that there is no school, Mrs. Whyte-Smith and Rusty and I spend many days picnicking in the woods and picking bluebells and blackberries. Annie makes delicious blackberry pies. I also like her rhubarb pies. One day we venture a bit further into the woods than usual, and Rusty begins to growl and pull at his lead. We soon discover the reason. In a small clearing up ahead we find a gypsy caravan, and another dog, a German shepherd who snarls at Rusty, and Rusty snarls back. The two dogs approach each other warily, sniff around a bit, pace and growl a bit more, and then decide to ignore each other. The caravan is brightly painted in squiggles made up of all colors of the rainbow. White smoke is coming out of a little chimney at the top of the caravan, and a toothless old woman is sitting on the step by the door, shelling peas into a bowl. Mrs. Whyte-Smith says good afternoon to her, but she merely stares at us and doesn't answer.

When we come back to Morley Manor, Mrs. Whyte-Smith tells the Colonel about the gypsy caravan. He becomes very angry and warns her never to go that far into the woods again. "They are dirty foreigners," he says, "they could be German spies." Mrs. Whyte-Smith just pats his hand and laughs. "Rubbish, my dear," she says. "What rot!"

Several days later, when we go deep into the woods again and look for the caravan, it is no longer there. The only sign that the gypsies have been there is the flattened grass at the edge of the clearing where the caravan had stood and a scrap of paper snagged in the deeper grass under the trees.

A few days later we drive to Chertsey and meet Andy who is still stationed nearby on an American military base. Mrs. Whyte-Smith leaves me at the cinema to watch some Mickey Mouse and Donald Duck cartoons because she has to go somewhere with Andy. Afterward we go for tea again in Ye Olde Tea Shoppe and Andy gives me some more gum. On the ride home Mrs. Whyte-Smith is very quiet, but I can tell she's happy. She keeps humming to herself all the way home.

Mimi writes that if she weren't living so far away she would come to visit me. I'm already forgetting what Mimi and Ephraim and Erika look like. I asked Mimi to send me a photograph and she said she would try. I've already sent her a photo of me and Rusty that Annie took with my Brownie camera.

Every night before I fall asleep, I try to remember Mama's and Papa's and Oma's faces. It's getting more and more difficult to remember what they look like. After I recite the Shema, I tell God: "Even though the *goyim* are very nice to me and I'm quite happy here, I would like to see my parents again. How long do You expect this war to last?"

*   *   *

School starts again, and before we know it winter is here and it's Christmas 1940. I am quite ill during the holidays and unable to celebrate with the Colonel, Mrs. Whyte-Smith, and Annie, as I did last year. This is the first time I have anything more serious than a cold and I'm running a high fever. Mrs. Whyte-Smith calls

Thorpe's only doctor, Dr. Morgan, who comes and looks into my throat and listens to my chest. He says I have a throat infection together with a bad case of bronchitis and must stay in bed and drink lots of fluids. He instructs Mrs. Whyte-Smith to boil a pot of hot water, put my head over the steaming pot, cover my head with a large towel so as to make a tent, and have me inhale the steam. Mrs. Whyte-Smith and Annie make a big fuss over me. I can tell they are very worried. Every few minutes one of them comes into my room to check on me, to feel my head, to take my temperature, to bring me something to drink. I am too tired and weak even to read. Sometimes Mrs. Whyte-Smith sits next to my bed and reads to me from *Great Expectations* until I drop off to sleep. I also like her to read from the Pollyanna books. I admire Pollyanna tremendously for always finding reasons to be glad about everything even though she's had such rotten luck.

One night, while my temperature is running very high, I dream about Papa. In my dream I can't see his face because, as usual, his head is covered with his *tallis*, and just a little bit of the black tefillin box that is strapped to his head peeps out. He's praying, swaying backward and forward. Although I can hear his voice, I can't make out the words. I try to get his attention. *Papa, Papa, it's me, Friedl. Look, I'm over here.* But he ignores me and continues *davening*.

Luckily we have only a few air-raids while I'm sick, and Annie wraps a blanket around me and helps me down to the shelter where I just lie on the bench dozing until the all-clear sounds and I'm able to crawl back into my bed. I stay in bed for three weeks before the fever goes down, and after that I'm so weak I can barely walk. Annie says, "My goodness, ducky, you gave us quite a scare. Now we've got to fatten you up 'coz you're thinner than a rail." Mrs. Whyte-Smith is so relieved that I'm better that while I'm regaining my strength she allows me to sit in her *chaise longue* in the drawing room, tucked in with a blanket and some books, with a fire blazing in the grate despite the coal rationing and plenty of Cadbury biscuits and hot tea at my side. Rusty, too, seems to have been worried, for during my convalescence he rarely leaves my side. The drawing room is normally out of bounds for him, but when he knows I'm in there he continually whines and growls and scratches the door with his paws so that Mrs. Whyte-Smith finally relents and lets him come in. He immediately curls up next to me so that I can play with his ears and stroke him from time to time, and goes to sleep. The Colonel, too, is pleased to see me up and about again. He pokes his head into the drawing room and gruffly says, "So, you're better, eh what?"

When I return to school in the middle of February, the whole class gives me a big welcome and Mr. Anderson makes sure I get the seat nearest the stove. Then he gives me the wonderful news that while I was ill the bully boys were sent away.

* * *

Dear Frieda:

I'm so happy to hear that you're feeling better and are back in school. I was very worried about you. I'm very excited because I just got a letter from Ephraim and he says his hostel is going to let me come and live there. This will be the first time they've let any girls in, and it's all because Ephraim kept nagging the committee until they finally gave in. Every Wednesday night when the committee met, Ephraim burst into the room and begged them, "Take my sisters from the *goyim*."

I'll let you know the exact date I'm moving. We first have to get permission from the Perlows, because they're still in charge of me. In a way, I'll be sad to leave the Evanses because they've been very nice to me, but I won't miss the pigs or the dogs. Right now Mr. and Mrs. Evans are grieving because their son's submarine was torpedoed in the North Sea. Officially, he's listed as "missing in action," but they don't believe there were any survivors. The house is very sad and gloomy and they go about their work with heavy hearts. I feel very sorry for them.

Love and kisses,
Mimi

* * *

Dear Mimi:

I was very happy to hear your news and that you'll soon be in Cardiff with Ephraim. I was sorry to hear about the Evanses' son. What rotten luck.

I am also moving, but I'm not happy about it. Annie has been called up. She's joining the ATS. Colonel and Mrs. Whyte-Smith say they can't live in Morley Manor without a maid. They're selling the house and moving to a smaller house in Croydon. Mrs. Whyte-Smith says she would love to take me along but I have to stay in Thorpe as long as the Simmonses are still in charge of me. Anyway, she says she wouldn't be able to look after me without Annie's help. They've found a new home for me in Thorpe, on Coldharbour Lane, with Mr. and Mrs. Thorndike. The Thorndikes have a little baby. I am going to meet them for the first time tomorrow.

Annie tried on her ATS uniform for me and I told her how spiffing she looks in it. I know I'm going to miss her and Mrs. Whyte-Smith and the Colonel a lot. I'm especially sad to leave Rusty. Mrs. Whyte-Smith says Croydon is not far and she'll try and motor over with Rusty to visit me if she gets some extra petrol.

Love from your sister,
Frieda

* * *

Dear Mimi:

The Thorpe post office sent me your letter. I am now living at The Rising. I was glad to hear you are in Cardiff in the hostel with Ephraim.

The Rising is even larger than Morley Manor. Mr. and Mrs. Thorndike have a little boy, Wilfred. He is a year old and just learning to walk. He's a very nice little baby but cries a lot. The Thorndikes have lots and lots of land. I am learning to play croquet. They also have stables and horses and I'm learning to ride. The horse I'm learning on is called Strawberry. Yesterday, Strawberry kept snorting and shying, which made me very nervous. Mr. Thorndike said Strawberry might be coming down with something. Mrs. Thorndike is a champion rider and has won many awards for steeplechase. The mantelpiece in the library is covered with a lot of cups and ribbons. Mrs. Thorndike is blond and thin and very pretty. During the day she always dresses in a riding habit.

I'll write again soon.

Love from your sister.

*   *   *

Dear Mimi:

It's a bit far for me to walk to school now so Mr. Thorndike takes me there in his car every day on his way to Guilford where his office is. After school I usually walk back unless Mr. Thorndike finishes work early and picks me up. He drives a beautiful big black shiny Bentley. The Thorndikes must be very rich. They have a butler, two maids, and a groom for the horses. They are lucky that the maids are too old to be called up. I think the butler is also too old, but I'm not sure. His name is George and he told me to call him Mr. George. All he does all day is polish the silver. Actually, one of the maids, Gwen, comes from Wales, from Merthyr Tydfil. I think it's a mining town near Cardiff. Isn't that a coincidence? She speaks with a Welsh accent which sounds a bit like she's singing. I have a hard time understanding her. The other maid, Maggie, is ancient and doesn't do very much work. She worked for Mrs. Thorndike's mother before Mrs. Thorndike was even born, so she's been in the family forever. I eat all my meals in the kitchen with the maids and Mr. George. Gwen says I have very good table manners for a refugee.

I don't know if I told you that my friend Millie went back to London. Her parents missed her too much and they said if the bombing started again they would try and find a place in the country where they could all be together.

Love and kisses,

Your sister Frieda

*   *   *

Dear Mimi:

I have bad news. I'm leaving the Thorndikes after only a few weeks. The other day I noticed a bowl of chocolate Easter eggs on the sideboard in the front hall. Each one was wrapped in different colored shiny paper and I took one. One of the maids, or Mr. George, I don't know who, saw me and told Mrs. Thorndike. She called me into the library and told me, "I will not tolerate stealing. You are obviously nothing but a little Jewish thief." She told Mr. Anderson and he's found another family for me in Staines called Howell. I will send you my new address as soon as I can.

Love,

Your sister, Frieda

* * *

Dear Mimi:

I am now in Staines with the Howells. The Howells live in a small house on a street where all the houses look the same. They have a little boy called Anthony who is four years old. They call him Tony for short. Tony has taken a liking to me, probably because I like playing with him. I also share a bedroom with him and in the mornings he wakes up very early and jumps into my bed to cuddle and play. There is also a dog called Penny, a black and white terrier with ears that stand up. They called him Penny because when he was a puppy he swallowed one. He is a very friendly dog but he's not Rusty.

Please write soon.

Your loving sister, Frieda

*   *   *

Throw Your Feet Over Your Shoulders

Dear Mimi:

 The Howells don't have a car but Mr. Howell has a motor-cycle, which he rides to work. He's a mechanic in the army, but they let him live at home and not on the army base. He doesn't even have to wear a uniform. One day, Mr. Howell gave me a ride on the back of his motorcycle. It was very exciting, but he says he can't go joy-riding too often because petrol is rationed. The Howells like to have fun. In the evenings they pull back the carpet, turn on the wireless or put some records on the gramo-phone and dance the fox-trot, quick-step and waltz. Sometimes, Mrs. Howell's sister and brother-in-law come over and the four of them dance together. I love to watch them. Mr. Howell tried to teach me the quick-step. We must have made a funny looking pair because he's so tall and had to bend over so I could reach his shoulder. I kept stepping on his toes but he didn't mind, just laughed and told me I have two left feet. When they're not dancing, they play a card game called Whist, which looks very complicated.

 I have to go to bed now.

 Love from your sister, Frieda

*   *   *

Dear Mimi:

The Howells grow a lot of vegetables in their garden and they let me help with the hoeing and weeding and watering. They also have some rabbits. Mr. Howell takes care of them. I love to pet the rabbits and feed them lettuce. The other night Mrs. Howell made a delicious chicken stew for supper but when we were finished she told me it was really rabbit stew. This made me feel a bit ill, especially when on the next day I saw how Mr. Howell kills them. He holds the rabbit up by its feet and keeps hitting it on the back of the neck with the blunt edge of an axe until it is dead. I was especially sad because it was the white rabbit I used to pet a lot. Mrs. Howell also makes a fish called prawns. Do you know if rabbits and prawns are kosher animals?

I take a bus to St. Mary's school in Thorpe every day because I didn't want to go to a new school in Staines, and anyway I need permission from Mr. and Mrs. Simmons if I want to change schools. I'm glad Mr. Anderson is still my teacher.

Please write soon,

Love,

Your sister Frieda

* * *

Dear Mimi:

I only just received your letter. Last week I had my tonsils out. I was getting too many infections so Mrs. Howell wrote to Mrs. Simmons and got her permission to get my tonsils out. Mrs. Howell took me to Windsor Hospital by bus and we sat and waited in the out-patient department until it was my turn. Mrs. Howell told me they have no spare beds in the main hospital because they're all filled with wounded soldiers. The nurse put a mask over my mouth and nose and told me to count backward from a hundred and the next thing I knew I woke up on a mattress on the floor. I was in a lot of pain and started being sick all over the place. There were some other children lying near me also being sick. One little girl started to cry but then she stopped because it probably hurt too much to cry. I didn't cry at all.

Mrs. Howell took me back home by bus. I was sick all over the bus also and the bus conductor was very angry. When we got into the house, I smelled bacon frying and was sick all over again, but Mrs. Howell was very nice about it. She told me to get into bed and then brought me up some ice cream which was the only thing I could swallow. Penny was happy to see me and jumped all over me. I've decided I like him just as much as Rusty. He seemed to know that I was in pain and curled up at the foot of my bed just like Rusty used to do. Tony has also been very nice to me even though he is so little. He brings me my ice cream and my books. My throat was very sore for a few days but now I'm starting to feel better.

Love from your sister,
Frieda

*   *   *

A few months after my tonsillectomy, I receive a letter from Mimi. She writes that she will be staying in London with the Perlows for a few days and will come to visit me. I am very excited. The Howells have given Mimi permission to take me to the flicks. When I open the door, I barely recognize her. It's been over two years since we last saw each other in London before the war, and so much has happened since then to both of us. She's grown taller and now has a bust. We can't stop hugging each other. Mimi tells Mrs. Howell that she's taking me to the Odeon in Staines.

We walk to the High Street, holding hands, and as we cross the little bridge over the Thames Mimi says, "Oh look, there's my friend Mr. Gottlieb in his car. Perhaps he'll give us a lift." We get into the back of a little black Triumph, and Mimi introduces me to her friend Mr. Gottlieb. He's a middle-aged man with a beard and glasses and wears a black homburg. From under his hat I notice the edge of a black velvet yarmulke peeking out. It is a long time since I've seen anyone who looks and dresses like Mr. Gottlieb, and a pleasant sense of recognition flutters in my stomach. Mr. Gottlieb drives and Mimi and I chatter away in the backseat. After a few minutes I say, "Mimi, wasn't that the Odeon we just passed?" Mimi says, "We're going to a different Odeon, Friedl."

We drive and drive and pass two more cinemas called Odeon, and each time Mimi says the same thing. "We're going to a different Odeon, Friedl." After driving for more than an hour, we arrive at Paddington Railway Station in London. Mr. Gottlieb says goodbye to us at the entrance to the station and Mimi thanks him and then leads me to a platform where a train is waiting. On the doors of the train in large letters that cannot be missed are the words *Cardiff, Wales*.

A feeling of great excitement rushes over me. For as soon as I see the train and those words *Cardiff, Wales*, I know immediately that Mimi is taking me to my brother, and that the three of us will be together for the first time since leaving Vienna almost three years ago. When the train begins to move, Mimi puts her arm around me. She says Mrs. Simmons refused to grant permission for me to move to the Cardiff hostel. And so Mimi had to come and take me away secretly, without letting me know ahead of time. She says that she and Ephraim decided I had lived with *goyim* long enough. They even kept their plans secret from Rabbi Schonfeld, in case he didn't approve or would insist on them telling the Simmonses.

Then Mimi tells me that everyone in the Cardiff hostel calls her by her Hebrew name, Miriam, and that is what she wants me to call her from now on. Then we both start singing "Underneath the Spreading Chestnut Tree" and "The White Cliffs of Dover" and other popular songs. I'm amazed at how matter-of-factly I have accepted this development. It's as if I've known all along, even as we rode in Mr. Gottlieb's car, what is going to happen. And perhaps deep down in my heart I did.

CHAPTER FOUR

CARDIFF

I was naturally very happy to be reunited with my brother, though I barely recognized him and felt a little strange with him at first. He had grown several inches. His face was much thinner, emphasizing his cheekbones. His forehead and nose had also become more prominent, and his hair, which had been a light auburn, had darkened. In addition, he now wore glasses, wire-rimmed and ill-fitting. The bridge of his glasses was constantly slipping down his nose and he was constantly pushing it up with his index finger. On his head he wore an English schoolboy's peaked cap, under which his *peyos* were still folded behind his ears. He didn't embrace me as he had when we parted three years before. I suppose he felt that such physical displays of affection were no longer appropriate now that he was almost twelve years old.

Ephraim's joy at our reunion must have been even greater than mine, because it was through his efforts that his sisters were removed from gentile homes and brought back to *Yiddishkeit*. Miriam told me that after Mr. Gottlieb left us at Paddington Station, he telephoned the Howells and told them that I wouldn't be coming back. After their initial shock, they were very understanding and even forwarded me a parcel containing my clothes and books and, most important, my gas mask.

The morning after my arrival at the Cardiff hostel the police appeared. They were sent by Mrs. Simmons, who became livid when she learned what had happened. She told the police that I had been kidnapped. Two serious-looking Welsh "bobbies" took me into a room. I was very nervous. They asked me if I had been coerced into coming to Cardiff or if I had made the journey of my own free will. On the other side of the door, Miriam and Ephraim waited for my answer with bated breath. They did not know how I would respond. When I emerged from the room and they realized that I had told the bobbies that of course I came of my own free will, they let out huge sighs of relief. Somehow the press got hold of the story of my "kidnapping" and it was written up in some of the afternoon newspapers as a minor *cause célèbre* which, while creating a welcome distraction from the grim war news, was hardly sensational and lasted barely a day.

Rabbi Schonfeld was notified and was not at all upset; in fact, he seemed pleased that the three of us had found a way to be together. Somehow he must have managed to pacify Mrs. Simmons, because she never bothered us again.

The three of us lived together in the Cardiff hostel for about eighteen months, until the hostel closed down, probably for lack of funds. This was my first experience of communal life, but I adjusted rapidly because I was with my brother and sister. The matron of the hostel, Mrs. Z., had taken a special interest in Ephraim when he first arrived, partly because he suffered frequent bouts of bronchitis and needed extra care. Mrs. Z. and her husband were childless refugees from Poland, and when Miriam and I arrived, they took us under their wing, as well.

I was enrolled in a Cardiff school for girls and had to wear a uniform provided by the hostel's invisible committee: a pleated navy tunic, white blouse, and navy blazer with the school shield on the breast pocket stitched in the school colors, navy and yellow. The shield prominently and proudly proclaimed the school's Latin motto, *Semper Sersum*, "Always Upward." To top it off, there was a wide-brimmed navy felt hat with a navy and yellow grosgrain ribbon around the brim. Once again, I found myself the only Jewish girl in my form and sometimes the object of overt anti-Semitism from both students and teachers. (My English teacher announced to our class of nine- and ten-year-olds: "Being that Frieda is *German*, I find it a bit strange that she's never heard of Goethe...")

One of the girls in my form spread a rumor about me that swept like wildfire through the class, and eventually throughout the whole school. She had seen me scratching my hand and told everyone that I must have scabies because I was a "dirty Jew." All the girls moved away from me when they saw me approach, afraid of catching this contagious condition, and the girls sitting near me in class insisted on moving their desks until I was left sitting in the center of the room, completely isolated as if marooned on a desert island. As a result, the headmistress called me into her office and insisted that I undergo an examination by the school nurse. She found that I did not have scabies, of course, but the rumor that I was a "dirty Jew" stuck.

Every morning there was a school assembly at which prayers were recited and hymns sung. There were two other Jewish girls in the school, both in the upper forms, and the three of us had to wait outside the hall until the religious part of the assembly was over. Then the doors were flung open, and with hundreds of eyes upon us, watching and waiting, the three of us were invited to join our respective classes and listen to announcements from the headmistress. As the youngest of the three girls and in the lowest form, I had to walk the entire length of the assembly hall in order to reach my class. I felt hundreds of hostile eyes on me (or so it seemed), as I made my way down, with the whole school waiting for me to take my place. Every morning was torture anew.

The bright spot in my school life was the emphasis on sports and gymnastics, at which I excelled. I quickly learned the Welsh sport of lacrosse and qualified for my class team. My standing in sports had the effect of somewhat blunting the anti-Semitic attitude of some of my classmates, at least to my face, and when I flew down the field wielding my lacrosse stick I was able, for a short time, to forget the daily torment of the school assemblies. Eventually I became so accustomed to the routine that the assemblies hardly bothered me. It also helped that at the end of the school day I was able to come home to a Jewish environment and to my sister and brother.

The hostel was housed in a three-story private home situated on a busy thoroughfare, Cathedral Road, which had a tramline running through it. About thirty children of all ages, mostly boys, lived in the hostel. Some of the older boys were already out of school and working. Because of wartime rationing, our meals were meager and the cook had to be very creative. One Shabbos, for instance, we were served individual little birds, which were very tasty and tender; later we were told they were pigeons.

Mr. Z. set the tone for religious observance. On Shabbos he led the *davening* in one of the downstairs rooms where a thick, wooden *mechitzah* was erected to separate the boys from the girls. Friday nights and Shabbos lunch were uplifting occasions, despite the food shortage. Mr. Z. made *Kiddush*, and after we had eaten, we sang traditional *zemiros*. It carried me back to our Friday nights at home in Vienna when Papa and Erika used to sing in harmony. Mr. Z. was very learned and gave *shiurim*, lessons in Talmud, to the boys. During the week, after school, volunteer tutors, Jewish residents of Cardiff, arrived to give us Hebrew lessons. I learned to read Hebrew again and felt a great sense of accomplishment when I was able to *daven* and keep up with the other children.

Miriam suffered from excruciating pangs of guilt at having lived with *goyim* and eaten *treif.* After she arrived at the Cardiff hostel she became very *frum*, very devout, and began to pray three times a day. Some of the boys, who must secretly have admired her long flaxen ringlets and buxom figure, often teased her and sang a Yiddish song whenever she entered the room: "*Oy iz dos a Rebbetzin!* – Oh what a Rebbitzin this is!" Miriam always refused to speak about her wartime experiences with the *goyim* and to this day becomes very agitated if the subject is brought up.

Mrs. Z. and her husband occupied a large bedroom on the second floor, and the three of us were often invited up to their room for a snack of toast and scrambled eggs, which Mrs. Z. prepared on a single electric plate. Because eggs were rationed, our scrambled eggs were made from egg powder. An invitation from Mrs. Z. to partake of *ersatz* scrambled eggs was always a special treat, and when I was seated on her down-covered bed, munching happily away, I had a sense of belonging and well-being such as I had not felt since leaving Vienna. And nothing had ever tasted more delicious than those powdered eggs.

In the Cardiff hostel I met Edith, who became my lifelong friend. She was a cheerful little girl with a good-hearted nature to go along with her dark blue laughing eyes. She seemed to wear a perpetual, contagious smile. Edith was the only child of a wealthy Hungarian cattle dealer. Her father traveled on business all over the world and had the wherewithal and ample opportunities to leave Europe. Alas, like so many others, he was unable to believe what was happening until it was too late and he could no longer leave. Luckily, he was able to spirit five-year-old Edith out of the country with one of his sisters. Edith and her aunt made it to Belgium just as that country was being overrun by the Nazis, and they barely managed to sail on one of the last boats to leave Ostend for England.

Edith and I regularly took the No. 4 tram to Roath Park, where we practiced hitting tennis balls against a wall with some old rackets we found lying around. Eventually we moved onto real courts and thus began my lifelong love affair with the game of tennis. At other times the two of us concocted plays and skits and dressed up in anything we could find for the performances we put on for the other children and adults in the hostel. I still wonder at the fortitude and enthusiasm with which they received our silly, childish productions.

*   *   *

On December 7, 1941, not long after I arrived in Cardiff, we learned that the United States had entered the war. Newsreels showed the American ships on fire in Pearl Harbor after the Japanese surprise attack. There was great excitement in the hostel amid speculation that the war would soon be over now that the Americans had joined the fight. Alas, it did not take long for us to realize that the war in Europe had nothing much to do with what was going on in the Pacific, on the other side of the world, and that Hitler's conquering rampage was barreling forward unabated.

Just before the Cardiff hostel closed down, my brother became a bar mitzvah. On Shabbos, after *davening*, we made *Kiddush* over some raisin wine and toasted him with a *l'chaim*. The only other symbol of celebration was a cake on which was inscribed in Hebrew the famous quotation from Jeremiah 31:19: *Is not Ephraim my dearest son?* Soon after his bar mitzvah, Ephraim left to study in a newly established yeshiva (in Staines, coincidentally), where he remained for several years. (While in yeshiva, Ephraim occasionally sent me his socks to darn, and I silently blessed and thanked Mrs. Whyte-Smith for having taught me this useful skill.)

By this time we were no longer receiving mail from our parents. In the spring of 1941 the Nazis invaded Yugoslavia and all communication between us ceased.

In 1942, my sister Esther (by then Erika had also assumed her Hebrew name) married a simple, gentle man, also a Viennese refugee, who somehow managed with great patience and good humor to tolerate her strange habits and dreamy temperament. The match, the *shidduch*, was engineered by Tante Regina. The couple lived in the East End of London, not far from the Simmons family, and twice survived the destruction of their dwelling, once by incendiary bombs and once by a direct hit from a v-2 rocket. Right after Esther's marriage, Tante Regina braved the torpedoes in the Atlantic and sailed for America.

During Miriam's stay in London, when she was on her way to Staines to "kidnap" me, she had lodged in the home of a Rabbi and Rebbetzin M., who lived in North London, not too far from Rabbi Schonfeld. It was on a Shabbos afternoon while she sat in the kitchen schmoozing with the Rebbetzin that she caught the eye of a young man who had to pass through the kitchen to reach another area of the house. On his part it seems to have been a case of love at first sight. Miriam was not yet fifteen, but was fully developed and had beautiful golden ringlets, enormous doe-shaped, sky-blue eyes, and a translucent complexion. Y. was twelve years her senior, a refugee from Poland. He was the only boy in a family of six girls, and I believe Miriam's looks must have reminded him of two of his sisters who reputedly were blonde beauties. As a boy, Y. had been considered a child prodigy in Jewish learning, a natural successor to his father, a prominent Chassidic rabbi in Lublin. In the summer of 1939, Y. was sent on a fund-raising mission to England, which is where he found himself stranded in September after the Nazis invaded Poland. Not one member of Y.'s family in Lublin survived the war.

The young man was so smitten with Miriam that he wanted to marry her on the spot. Rabbi Schonfeld, as our official guardian, obviously felt she was too young to marry and withheld his consent. When Miriam reached the legal marriageable age of sixteen, she no longer needed Rabbi Schonfeld's permission. And so, in 1943, my sister and Y. married. She told me years later that her main objective in marrying was to make a home for Ephraim and me. Alas, things didn't turn out quite the way she planned. Her husband, though a brilliant and charismatic Talmudic scholar and a successful businessman, later became one of the leaders of the fanatical Neturei Karta sect. Unfortunately, he was also dogmatic and demanding in their marriage and, over the years, trampled Miriam's gentle nature into almost catatonic submission. Mr. and Mrs. Z., who moved to London after the Cardiff hostel closed, were a great help and comfort to Miriam during the early years of her marriage. They had actually discouraged her from the union but were no match for the persuasive powers of Y.

CHAPTER FIVE

SHEFFORD

The Cardiff hostel closed in 1943, and Rabbi Schonfeld sent me to the village of Shefford in Bedfordshire to attend his Jewish Secondary School. The JSS was founded by his late father and had been evacuated to Shefford from London at the outbreak of the war. I was eleven years old and made the cross-country journey from Cardiff on my own, by train and motor coach. I was told that there would be someone to meet me at the Shefford bus stop. When I climbed down from the bus with my suitcase in one hand and my tennis racket in the other, I found waiting for me a very pretty girl with short, dark hair, and dimpled cheeks, who appeared to be around my age. She introduced herself as Pepi and helped me carry my belongings to the White House, a converted antique shop on Old Bridge Street, which was the school's headquarters; it had apparently acquired its name because of its whitewashed exterior.

As we walked, Pepi told me that she'd been born in Frankfurt and that she, too, had come to England on one of Rabbi Schonfeld's *Kindertransport*s. Like me, she had spent the first years of the war in gentile homes. She told me that what she missed most when she was living with *goyim* was not hearing *Kiddush* on Shabbat and *Havdalah* after Shabbat was over.

The White House was a low-standing, two-story building flanked on each side by similar structures. It contained the school's offices, one or two classrooms, and on the second floor, the welfare room, and surgery. A large, prefabricated Quonset hut had been erected on the grounds at the rear of the White House. The Hut served sometimes as the dining room, sometimes as the school's common room for all kinds of social activities. On Shabbat and Yom Tov it became the main shul.

Thus began for me the happiest two years of the war. Even though I was once again separated from my sisters and brother, I was now in a Jewish school with Jewish teachers and Jewish children. Most of the children were billeted with gentile families in Shefford and the surrounding villages, but those were merely their sleeping quarters. Rabbi Schonfeld placed me with a Jewish refugee couple, Mr. and Mrs. L., who had rented a house in Shefford in order to escape the London Blitz and not be separated from their two children, who had been evacuated with Rabbi Schonfeld's school. Soon after my arrival, I was overjoyed to be reunited with my Cardiff friend Edith, who also arrived in Shefford as a result of Rabbi Schonfeld's efforts. Edith became my roommate until the end of the war. The special bond Edith and I had forged in Cardiff was still there; it was as if we had never been separated. And though, over the years, we have sometimes lived on opposite sides of the world, that bond still remains as strong as ever.

When Rabbi Schonfeld's school first arrived in Shefford, most of the villagers greeted the children with unreserved enthusiasm and opened their hearts and homes to them. Some of the locals, however, were more tentative in their welcome: it was the first time they had ever seen a Jew, and they expressed surprise that the teachers and children did not have horns. At that time, the White House had not yet been acquired and no communal kosher dining facilities had been organized. The children had no choice but to eat in the homes of their gentile hosts. Most of the children came from Orthodox homes and many of them, only recently arrived from Europe, could not speak or understand very much English. They were rehearsed to tell their hosts, "We are fish-eating vegetarians," in the hope that this would prevent them from ingesting any real *treif*. Quite to the contrary, this resulted in a lot of confusion, because the villagers, only too happy to serve fish, placed plates of crabs and prawns and other shellfish before their young charges. There were a lot of puzzled expressions and hurt feelings when the children refused to eat the fish their hosts had so lovingly prepared.

The language barrier contributed to a lot of misunderstandings, but eventually the children learned the new language. The villagers became familiar with some of the Jewish customs and a very smooth relationship was forged between the villagers and the foreign "invaders." Rabbi Schonfeld met regularly with the local vicars and pastors, who were most cooperative in lending him their church facilities as classrooms and for other social events. I believe the close relationships that Rabbi Schonfeld established with the local clergy lasted well beyond the war years.

* * *

Unlike Thorpe, Shefford was not a pristine, picturesque English hamlet. I recall few thatched roofs and no village green. In fact, strictly speaking, Shefford was not even a village at all; at one time it had been a small market town, dating back to the year 1225, when it was granted a charter permitting it to hold a weekly market and an annual fair. Though country lanes abounded, it was in the surrounding areas, such as the villages of Clifton and Campton, and the nearby village of Meppershall with its castle ruins, that idyllic English country life as portrayed by Jane Austen and Charles Dickens could be found. Two narrow rivers with forgettable names, more like creeks really, ran through Shefford and eventually joined the River Ivel, which in turn flowed into the

Great Ouse to the north. On a hill on the outskirts of the village was a remarkable scenic outlook providing a panoramic view over the Ivel Valley. We discovered these facts and details by exploring and hiking in and around Shefford. In our history class we also learned that the name Shefford was derived from *Sheeps' Ford*, a reference to the sheep market that had at one time been held there and the ford that spanned the rivers.

One of the older girls, in writing a tribute to Rabbi Schonfeld many years later, said, "Shefford healed us." She was right. In Shefford we were all more or less on an equal footing, all refugees, all in the same boat, and we took care of each other. The knowledge that we were not alone in our experience, that we mattered to someone else, was part of our healing. To be sure, there were a few children in Shefford who had been lucky enough to escape from Europe with one or both parents, like the children of Mr. and Mrs. L., in whose home Edith and I were billeted, or the children of our headmistress, Dr. Judith Grunfeld, whose husband Dayan Grunfeld was a judge in the *Beit Din* (Jewish court) and traveled to and from London by train each day. But most of us were alone, without parents, and the shared experience of Shefford resulted in the kind of bond that goes beyond normal friendship and often transcends the relationship between siblings.

In all the time I spent in Shefford I never saw or knew of one incident of cruel bullying such as one hears goes on in schools today or, for that matter, has always gone on in British boarding schools. Sometimes, to be sure, we took out our frustrations on each other. Once, at supper, I found myself sitting across from Renate, a tall, beautiful dark-haired girl a couple of years my senior, who had a reputation for being quick-tempered. I must have been making a nuisance of myself in some way that annoyed her for she suddenly reached across the table and slapped my face. I was too stunned even to cry. I remember staring at this powerful, older girl opposite me with a hurt sort of puzzlement. Renate eventually apologized, but that was the worst indignity I ever suffered at the hands of a schoolmate in Shefford. (Today Renate has no memory of the incident, and when I visit Israel, where she lives, I usually look her up.)

Sheffordians, as we took to calling ourselves, are scattered all over the world, but when we meet, even sixty or more years later, that special bond is still there. The bond of healing.

My dear friend Marga, a refugee from Berlin, arrived in Shefford a few months after I did. Rabbi Schonfeld discovered her in the home of a farmer who was severely abusing her. This damaged, fragile girl became my friend when I was assigned to tutor her in Hebrew, not one word of which could she read or understand when she first arrived in Shefford. Marga shared her heart with me while we sat hunched over our books and homework assignments. As the months progressed and Marga's emotional wounds began to heal, she became the object of affection of one of the older boys, Martin, a Frankfurt refugee, with whom she exchanged sweet and innocent love letters. She and I composed some of her letters together with much giggling and mischievous plotting. Marga and Martin were Shefford's Romeo and Juliet, but their story had a much happier ending. Several years after the war, when we were back in London and had reached marrying age, Marga and Martin tied the knot in a simple ceremony performed by Rabbi Schonfeld. Marga discovered that her mother and sister had survived the war by hiding in Berlin right under the noses of the Nazis, and so she had the joy of having close family members present at her wedding. Marga and Martin's successful union lasted until Marga's death a few years ago, and Martin, unable to go on without his childhood sweetheart, followed soon after.

* * *

Our teachers were, for the most part, refugees like us. How Rabbi Schonfeld found the money to pay them is a mystery to this day, for obviously, none of us paid a penny in tuition. Yet we had textbooks to learn from, exercise books to write in, pencils, pens, blackboards, and chalk, not to mention all sorts of sports equipment. In addition, we had *siddurim* (prayer books), *Chumashim*,

(Five Books of Moses), and volumes of Talmud for the older boys. And when each boy became bar mitzvah, somehow, as if by magic, a pair of tefillin appeared. Parcels of secondhand clothes arrived regularly from various refugee committees, so that we were adequately clothed. What was most remarkable was that each of us received pocket money, one shilling per week, doled out by the matron, Miss D.

Dr. Judith Grunfeld, who had five children, lived in a house in the neighboring village of Campton, about a mile's walk from the White House. Every Shabbat she and the Dayan invited a few children to join their family and share their meager rations. It was a rare treat for us to sit at their Shabbat table and to hear the Dayan expound on that week's Torah portion. But it also gave us a very nostalgic and somewhat envious feeling to be at a Shabbat table with a mother and father and their children. Such normalcy was, for most of us, merely a bittersweet memory.

Dr. Grunfeld's elder daughter, Hannah, was at least two years younger than I and my other classmates, but because of her brilliance she was placed in my form, and the rest of us had a hard time keeping up with her. Dr. Grunfeld always bent over backward not to show any favoritism to her own children, sometimes, unfortunately, to their detriment. She expected more from them than from the rest of us and showed her disappointment if they did not measure up to her academic or behavioral standards.

Dr. Grunfeld was our queen. That, indeed, was the sobriquet we attached to her very early on: the Queen. To this day, old Sheffordians, in talking about Dr. Grunfeld among ourselves, always refer to her as "the Queen," which bewilders any outsider listening. (And if we throw in a reference to the White House, the listener is *really* befuddled.) It was not just that she was tall and had a regal, ramrod-straight bearing. There was an unmistakable, imperial air of aristocracy about her, an innate quality that cannot be acquired. The Queen also knew how to dress for dramatic effect. She always wore black with a lot of yellow or white accents, such as a yellow turban, from the front of which peeked a small swath of her dark, center-parted hair. The Queen's brown eyes were sharp, intelligent, and all-knowing. She could be harsh yet kind, strict yet compassionate, and ultimately, always fair. To sit in one of her *Tanach* (Bible) classes was a privileged experience not soon forgotten, for she was mesmerizing in her delivery, always in control of the class, and obviously passionate about her subject. No one would think of misbehaving or talking in her class.

I can still picture the Queen standing before our class in her black suit and yellow turban, her eyes alight with fervor, as she quoted from Isaiah 57:14 the passage that is read each Yom Kippur for the *Haftarah* portion after the Torah reading: "Clear the way, clear the way! Remove the obstacle from the path of My people." We spent the best part of an hour just on this one sentence, turning each Hebrew word over, this way and that, examining each syllable, establishing the root, the *shoresh* of each word, in an attempt to find out what the prophet meant and why this particular passage was chosen for the Yom Kippur *Haftarah* reading.

"What," the Queen asked, "is the path that must be cleared, and what is the obstacle the prophet is referring to?" She looked around the silent classroom; none of us had the answer. "It is the path between us and God, the path between God and us, the path of repentance. And the obstacle to true repentance is our behavior, our bad habits, which are hard to break, such as the habit of speaking *lashon hara*, spreading tales about our friends." Here the Queen paused, looking at each of us in turn to make sure that the message had sunk in. "It is not enough to abstain from food, to fast on Yom Kippur. We must remove all obstacles, such as unreasonable pride or lack of faith in God," she continued, "all of which must be cleansed from our hearts in order to achieve true repentance."

When I arrived in Shefford, the Queen was pregnant with her fifth child. One day we heard that she had gone into labor and rather than bother anyone, had driven herself to hospital where the baby was delivered. No one in Shefford, no member of her family, knew about it until it was all over. The Queen had, more than anything else, not wanted her husband in London to be notified and worry about her. She was our heroine and we were all in awe of her bravery. She was truly our Queen.

*   *   *

Because most of our teachers were from Germany, it was logical for the school's religious ideology to be based on the philosophy and teachings of Rabbi Samson R. Hirsch. The Grunfelds too were from Germany, from Frankfurt, and eventually, after the war, the Dayan published his commentary on Hirsch's famous work *The Chorev*. Many of the children in Shefford also came from German homes where Hirsch's philosophy had been a major force in their early upbringing. Other children, like me, came from Polish or Hungarian families, with Chassidic, Yiddish-speaking backgrounds. To the German Jews, or *Yekkes* as they are still called (a reference to the correct jacket attire always worn by a German Jew), Yiddish was a low-class, mongrel language, used by uneducated shtetl Jews or peasants, and Polish Jews were customarily looked down upon by *Yekkes* with condescension, even disdain. Yet somehow in Shefford our *Yekke* teachers managed to overcome this prejudice, and we all blended in and became one homogeneous group.

Every school day began with morning prayers in a small room at the back of the White House, then breakfast in the Hut, followed by an assembly of the whole student body. First we sang the school anthem, a passage from Psalm 119 beginning with "Your words are a light before my feet…," then we heard announcements. After assembly we had classes in Hebrew subjects until lunchtime: *Tanach*, Jewish history, conversational Hebrew, *Shulchan Aruch* (Jewish Law). The older boys had a separate class in Talmud with Rabbi Spitzer, a refugee from Hamburg who had managed to get out of Germany with his whole family. One of his daughters was also in my class. Besides our religious training, the teachers instilled in us a love for *Eretz Yisrael*, the Land of Israel, and that

94

inculcation prompted many Sheffordians to go on *hachsharah* (agricultural training in preparation for aliyah) after graduating, and later, after the State of Israel was established, to make aliyah and settle in Israel.

Though there was constant interaction between boys and girls of all ages, most of the relationships had an innocence, a brother-sister quality that no longer seems possible in today's social environment. There was never the slightest incident or whiff of sexual scandal in all the years that Rabbi Schonfeld's boys and girls lived in Shefford in such close quarters. To be sure there were one or two "couples," like Marga and Martin, who eventually married, but those relationships were rare and always conducted chastely and with utmost decorum.

The Queen's office was on the ground floor of the White House and she shared it with the unsalaried school secretary, Flora. Flora was a member of the wealthy Sassoon family of India, a branch of which had taken up residence for the duration of the war in a large mansion in Letchworth, a small town not far from Shefford. Flora had a high-pitched voice, almost at *Kopfstimme* level, and spoke in an Indian singsong with elongated vowels. As a result, she was a perfect object for our mimicry: "Will you pleee-ase goooo to the pooost ooooffice for me?"

Despite our mockery, we loved Flora and loved even more being invited to her home for Shabbat. She invited us on a regular basis, rotating so that everyone had at least one turn every few months. It was an intimidating experience to be waited on by Indian servants. Flora's father, Mr. Sassoon, encouraged the servants to listen in and partake of the *Kiddush*, after which they retreated silently behind our chairs, ready to serve us all the delicious curried dishes prepared by the Sassoon's Indian cook. We were all dumbstruck with awe on those occasions. As for me, I was in seventh heaven when Mr. Sassoon complimented me on my table manners, and I silently thanked and blessed Mrs. Whyte-Smith for having drummed them into me.

The teachers must have had many occasions to complain that they had not been paid. But when they entered the Queen's small office, the first thing that greeted their eyes was a huge framed sign above the mantelpiece that read, in bold letters that could not be missed: "**Those who never do more than they get paid for, never get paid for more than they do!**" Who would dare open his mouth and complain when confronted with this psychological ploy?

My favorite teacher was not a refugee but Mrs. Alice Klein, an Oxford-educated Englishwoman. It was rumored that Mrs. Klein's husband had deserted her years before, leaving her to support herself and her son by teaching English. Mrs. Klein invariably wore her black and purple Oxford gown when she taught. And teach she did – with such evident relish and gusto for her subject that it was impossible not to be infected by her enthusiasm. I can still see Mrs. Klein's round face, her dark, center-parted hair drawn back neatly into a chignon, glasses hovering over her nose, as she emoted lines from Wordsworth's famous poem, "Daffodils": *I wandered lonely as a cloud...*; or as she talked to us about the structure of Jane Austen's *Pride and Prejudice* and traced the progression of the conflict between Elizabeth Bennet and Mr. Darcy to its satisfactory resolution. Or, as she earnestly and often urged us to strive for *le mot juste* in our writing.

Alas, we didn't always appreciate Mrs. Klein as we should have. Some of our classes were held in various church halls, not only in the village of Shefford but in surrounding villages as well. My form met in the rectory of the church in Clifton, a village that lay a little over a mile from Shefford, a distance we usually walked four times a day: after breakfast, back for lunch, after lunch, and then back for supper. After lunch we had the option of taking a bus that arrived at a fixed time at the bus stop right opposite the White House. However, with wiles that any child will readily appreciate, we made it our business to dawdle so long over the *bentching*, the blessing after lunch, that often we missed the bus and had to walk. As a result, we also missed most of our first class of the afternoon. On the way to Clifton we dawdled some more, especially in the summer when we stopped to pick the wild blackberries that grew in profusion along the roadside. We were not allowed to hitch-hike; there were vague rumors floating around of a girl who had been attacked a couple of years earlier by a lorry driver who had picked her up hitchhiking to Luton. We did hitchhike, of course, sometimes even flagging down the Queen's little Morris Minor before we realized whose car it was. She was always good-natured about it though, even as she reprimanded us and invited as many of us as she could fit in to pile into her car.

How much grief we must have given Mrs. Klein when we decided to play truant one afternoon and hide under the pews of the Clifton church. Poor Mrs. Klein! I remember peering out from my hiding place and seeing her standing forlornly at the entrance to the church, her black and purple gown billowing around her in the breeze as she called tremulously, "Children, children, I know you are in there. Now, please come out."

At the beginning of 1945 the war was winding down and we were sometimes allowed to go down to London. The film *Henry V* with Laurence Olivier had just come out and was playing in the West End, and Mrs. Klein received permission from the Queen to take our form to London to see it. I believe Mrs. Klein paid for our train fares and cinema tickets out of her own pocket. What an outing that was! We had read through the play in class before-hand to familiarize ourselves with the language and plot, and in the cinema I found myself mouthing the words silently along with the characters on the screen. *We few, we happy few, we band of brothers/For he today that sheds his blood with me/Shall be my brother...* As our blacked-out train chugged back to Shefford through the darkness, each of us tried to outdo the other, declaim-ing lines from the play until we were hoarse. Toward the end of the journey, I noticed that Mrs. Klein had become withdrawn and sat silent in the corner of the compartment, not really listening to us, her thoughts obviously elsewhere. Was she, I wondered, thinking of her errant husband? I never found out.

(Many years later, when I myself was teaching high-school

English, the syllabus called for a Shakespeare tragedy and I chose *Macbeth* for my class to study, purely because that is the play I best remembered from my days in Mrs. Klein's class. And as I taught and the play unfolded, I thought of Mrs. Klein with gratitude and nostalgia.)

Most of our teachers were dedicated, capable, and driven to impart knowledge. Some, however, were not qualified to teach young children. This was quite obvious even to our young and inexperienced eyes. Many of them had been given their teaching jobs as an act of kindness, because they needed the work and also, probably, because they worked for less pay than more qualified teachers. For instance, our French teacher, Dr. E., had been a university professor in his native Hamburg and had no experience with children our age, who often talked and misbehaved in class. He was long-winded and pedantic, and accustomed to giving lectures to adults; he had never had to deal with discipline problems. To make matters worse, the poor man was myopic. He wore very thick glasses, and held the textbook right up to his nose when he read. As a result, we mocked him mercilessly behind his back and tormented him in class by playing cruel tricks on him. I often developed a mysterious cough with which I disrupted his class, forcing him to send me out of the room. Once outside, I would immediately open *The Girls' Crystal* or one of the books I had borrowed from Shefford's limited library.

Another teacher, Mr. G., a gentle refugee from Frankfurt, was supposed to teach us conversational Hebrew. We could tell that he was a fish out of water in the classroom. He used every excuse to get out of teaching, and at the slightest sign of talking or misbehavior on our part would declare, "Because of that you don't deserve to be taught by me today!" With that, he'd march to his desk, snap open his newspaper, and hide behind it for the remainder of the period, leaving us to our own devices. That was all the encouragement that I, for one, needed. I slipped the ever ready magazine or book from my satchel and was transported to another world for fifty blissful minutes.

On the other hand, our math teacher, Mrs. J., was overly conscientious, not only in teaching her subject, which she drilled into us ruthlessly (in my case to no avail!); she was also a fanatic about good posture. She was a big, hefty woman, who walked around the classroom, where we sat on backless benches at trestle tables, hunched over our textbooks. When we least expected it, she would pound into the small of our backs with her hammerlike fist, exclaiming, "Sit up straight, child!" The thump could be heard clear across the room, and it is a wonder that the poor victim did not go flying over the table and escaped with spine intact. In order to avoid this painful experience, we learned to anticipate Mrs. J.'s progress around the room and sat up straight before she could go on the attack. As a result, many of us eventually did learn to sit up straight without prompting.

Mrs. J. had a son who was in love with Rike, one of the older girls. Rike's posture, not to mention her aptitude in geometry, must have been up to Mrs. J.'s exacting standards, because this was another couple whose romance blossomed in Shefford. Like Marga and Martin, they too married in London some years after the war.

*   *   *

A great part of our Shefford experience took place on the Meadow, a field that a generous local farmer lent to the school. On the Meadow we held all our sports events: handball, volleyball, field and track races. The Meadow provided a great outlet for our high spirits, our energy, our frustrations. While working out on the Meadow, we could forget the war. All sadness and loneliness, all speculation as to the fate of our parents was temporarily shelved as we concentrated on running and jumping, throwing and catching and hitting the ball.

We were divided into two houses, British boarding school style, Hermon House and Carmel House, and the houses competed against each other. I became a hurdle jumper, and I loved playing shinty (a sport much like field hockey but much rougher). It was during a game of shinty, while I was dribbling the ball with my shinty stick, that I earned my nickname. My classmate Malka, the granddaughter of the Belzer Rebbe, was, like me, pretty wild on the field, and she suddenly yelled, "Pass me the ball, Friddles!" The name stuck.

Once or twice a year we had a Sports Day, when Rabbi Schonfeld came up from London to hand out prizes to the winners of various sports events and races. Once, after Rabbi Schonfeld's marriage, he even persuaded his father-in-law, the chief rabbi of the British Empire, Rabbi Hertz, to present the prizes. When Rabbi Schonfeld handed us our prizes he always had something personal to say. His memory was prodigious, not just for our names but for many details of our lives. Rarely did anything escape him. On one such prize day, I went up to receive a trophy from him for the hundred-meter hurdle race, which I had won. He shook my hand with one hand and with the other handed me my trophy. "Well done, Frieda," he said, and then, out of the blue, he asked, "Do you still speak Yiddish?" I was flabbergasted, and too ashamed to admit that I had forgotten almost all my Yiddish. Before I could say anything, he beat me to it. In Yiddish he said, "Throw your feet over your shoulders and run away!" Then his beard began to wobble in that old remembered way and he couldn't stop laughing, and I, of course, joined in. Then he added, in English, "You certainly did a good job today, young lady, keep it up!"

* * *

A young, handsome, charismatic teacher, Meyer Eisemann, originally from Frankfurt, taught *Chumash*. We called him by his nickname, "Bubu." Because of his incredible musical talent, Bubu also taught music theory and appreciation. He spent a lot of time on useless information about diminished thirds and augmented fifths as if he expected us all to become virtuosos, but we didn't mind and studied hard to do well in his classes. (He confided in me years later that he was totally ignorant of music theory and was barely able to stay one chapter ahead of the class!) Besides being so good-looking, Bubu had long, sensitive fingers, the hands of a musician. All the girls, including me, were in love with him.

I was proud to excel in Bubu's *Chumash* class. I remember particularly learning the Torah portion entitled *Bo*, the section in *Shemot* (*Exodus*) dealing with some of the ten plagues and a pharaoh who kept changing his mind about letting the Israelites leave Egypt. Bubu gave us a written test on the *parashah*, part of which consisted of having us translate certain passages. Just before the plague of locusts is brought down on the Egyptians, there is a sentence (10:8) that reads: "And [Moses] was brought back again unto Pharaoh…" I was the only one in the class to translate the sentence correctly; everyone else translated it as "[Moses] came back again…" The Torah uses the *pu'al binyan*, the passive past tense conjugation of the verb "to return." Thus did I earn, to my eternal pride and shock, and for the first and last time, a higher mark than the Queen's daughter!

Bubu also wrote and produced our musical plays. Soon after I arrived in Shefford, in an effort to make me feel at home, Bubu gave me the starring role of Queen Esther in a Purim operetta he had written. I was totally unsuited for the part. Not only did I have blond hair where the Persian queen's must have been black, but I also had no voice and could barely carry a tune. Another girl, Mariette, who had dark hair and a lovely voice had been hankering for the part and was naturally peeved; I don't think she ever forgave me for usurping the role that should rightfully have been hers. One of the verses I had to sing to the boy playing King Ahashuerus was:

I am Esther ruler great,
My father poor of the cobbler's trade
Will try to please your majesty,
If he tries you'll surely see.

Bubu had a phonograph, hand-cranked of course, on which he played records of classical symphonies and operas for us. Because of Bubu, we learned to recognize the works of Beethoven and Schubert, Mozart and Dvorak, and to appreciate the operas of Verdi and Puccini. The opening bars of Beethoven's Fifth Symphony became the Shefford signature tune, which we whistled to summon each other. Bubu taught us to recognize the different musical instruments and sections that make up a symphony orchestra: the strings, woodwinds, percussion. He had us draw a diagram showing the position of each instrument, starting with the first violin just in front of the conductor's podium, and going all the way up and back to the kettle drums, cymbals, and triangle. Bubu also formed and conducted the school choir in three voices. Not only did we sing Hebrew songs, we also learned classical pieces such as "Hail the Conquering Hero" from Handel's oratorio *Judas Maccabeus*.

Shabbat was, of course, a great time for singing. And sing we did, led by Bubu, at the Friday night dinner and Shabbat lunch tables, and then again later, at an *oneg Shabbat*, with the girls on one side of the Hut and the boys on the other, and dusk settling in so that we could barely make out each other's faces. We sang our hearts out with songs like "*Heveinu Shalom Aleichem*" and "*Hinei Ma Tov.*" The message of "*Hinei Ma Tov*" was not lost on us: "How good it is for brothers to dwell together in peace."

Much later, after the war, Bubu became an impresario for a short time and put on concerts at the Royal Albert Hall, to which we were all, naturally, invited.

Chanukah in Shefford was a magical time. We put on our usual plays and skits, of course, but each night of the eight-day festival the boys' menorahs lit up the Hut. We had to take special care not to create a fire hazard and, in addition, not allow a chink of light to escape through the thick blackout coverings over the windows. Some of the boys had brought menorahs with them from their homes in Europe. (I can imagine a tearful father at the last moment frantically trying to find room in his boy's suitcase or rucksack to tuck a small menorah among clothes lovingly folded by a crying mother, with the solemn admonition not to lose it, to take care of it, and "Don't forget to think of us when you use it.") The menorahs were all lined up on trestle tables, and as another and another candle was added, the Hut became brighter and brighter until, by the eighth night, the whole room was ablaze with light. Bubu divided us into three groups and we sang every verse of *"Maʾoz Tzur"* in three-part harmony. On the eighth night, when we sang it for the last time, we repeated the last verse over and over again. We didn't want it to end. We didn't want to let go of the magic.

Perhaps there was a certain element of desperation in our singing. As if by shouting *Maʾoz Tzur* ("Our Strength, Our Rock, Our Salvation") loud enough and with enough fervor, we might reach God on His throne, knock Him off His pedestal, and get Him to come down and put everything to rights again. Certainly, none of us received any Chanukah presents – just our usual shilling pocket money – but I don't think we minded. Our hearts were too full of memories, memories of the Chanukahs we had spent in Vienna and Frankfurt and Cologne when our families were intact and before a little man with a funny mustache and a strange but all-too-familiar name had torn our lives asunder.

That first Chanukah after I arrived in Shefford it snowed for most of the week, and on the eighth night a heavy snowfall added to the drifts that were already on the ground. After singing *"Maʾoz Tzur"* for the last time, some of us ran outside and let go of our remaining energy in a free-for-all snowball fight. There was no traffic and we took over the whole street, yelling and sliding and falling in the snow, throwing and avoiding our little white missiles, and screaming when the ones we couldn't avoid went running icily down our backs. I recall a bunch of villagers grouped under a window opposite the White House. They were singing Christmas carols. Old Bridge Street was in total darkness because of the blackout, with only the whiteness of the snow relieving the blackness and creating an eeriness that to me was all too familiar. The moment the group began "Silent Night," I was taken back in memory to Thorpe and the carolers outside Morley Manor on Christmas Eve. With the strains of *"Ma'oz Tzur"* still ringing in my ears, I couldn't help but contrast the carolers and their Christmas songs with our choir and its Hebrew melodies. And though I didn't miss Christmas or the carols, I couldn't help noting the similarity of purpose. We each had our own way of praising the Almighty.

Around Chanukah time I also celebrated my twelfth birthday. *Celebrated* is not exactly the right word because, except for Edith and Marga, no one knew it was my birthday. Miriam and Ephraim both sent birthday cards. Miriam's card included a ten-shilling note, Ephraim's a bar of chocolate. I was now considered a bat mitzvah, alone answerable to God for my sins and behavior, and obligated to fast on Yom Kippur and other fast days throughout the year.

Seder nights were also joyous occasions in Shefford. A teacher presided at each end of the long, white-draped trestle tables; the youngest child at each table recited *"Mah Nishtanah...,* Why is this night different from all other nights of the year?" An indefinable nostalgia swept over each of us to temper our joy. Intermingled with our reciting of the Haggadah, the give and take of various commentaries, the singing, and the eating of matzos and other foods not served during the rest of the year, a certain melancholy intruded when we remembered former Pesachs at home. Only vaguely could I recall the last Pesach in Vienna: Papa sitting at the head of the table, wearing his white *kittle* and leaning against a pillow when he drank the wine. And Oma, who made the most delicious *matzah brei*, a fried matzah pancake made with eggs and dusted with sugar.

Was it at that last Seder in Shefford that it occurred to me how we all had the habit of starting our sentences in the same way, with either one of two phrases: "Before the war" (as in *Before the war, at home in Vienna…*; *Before the war we used to…*; *Once, in Berlin, before the war…*), or "After the war is over…"; "After things get back to normal…"; "After the fighting stops…"? Perhaps this differentiated the pessimists among us from the optimists – those whose frame of reference was nostalgia and those who looked to an inevitable future.

Still, I think it never entered any of our minds that the Allies might lose the war. Defeat was just not an option.

*   *   *

At the end of July school broke up for the six-week summer holiday. We had nowhere to go and so we stayed in Shefford. The teachers too remained, for they also had nowhere to go. Bubu organized picnic outings, and we spent a lot of time playing volleyball on the Meadow or Ping-Pong in the Hut. We also listened to a lot of classical music on his gramophone. Every now and then classes were given on various biblical topics, but attendance was voluntary. When we received our pocket money, we went by bus to the nearby towns of Bedford or Luton to see a picture. *Gone With the Wind* was a favorite, as were the Nelson Eddy–Jeannette MacDonald films like *Maytime*; war films like *Mrs. Miniver* and *Casablanca* also held us in thrall. Every now and then Bubu managed to get hold of some reels of pictures and then the Hut was turned into a cinema, with a small screen erected against one wall and a projector humming away and dependably breaking down. I spent a lot of time either on the Meadow or reading.

In the summer of 1944 Bubu and some of the other staff took us on a camping trip for two weeks. Boys and girls were separated and occupied different camping grounds not too far from each other. We slept in tents on thin straw palliasses, and it seemed to me that it rained for the whole two weeks. It must have been fine for one day, though, because I have a photograph that was taken at the camp, of Bubu surrounded by a gaggle of girls, each of us holding a tennis racket. I vaguely remember Bubu taking us to a park not far from the camping grounds, where we played on clay tennis courts until the rain started coming down again. The campsite was infested with all kinds of bugs and insects, and those that weren't crawling were flying. Mosquitoes abounded. The ground both inside and outside the tents was one squishy mess. I think we were all glad to get back to Shefford, and even happier when school started again in September.

Right after the new term began, the High Holy Days were upon us. This was a very solemn time in Shefford. On Rosh Hashanah and Yom Kippur we were more than ever conscious of our situation, and we prayed as never before for the safety of our parents and grandparents and other relatives; indeed, for all our Jewish brethren. The fervor with which I fasted and prayed that last Yom Kippur in Shefford is something I have never been able to experience since. I believe most of us felt a metaphysical longing that is impossible to convey in words. Through our tears we uttered the words, *Who will live and who will die; who by water and who by fire; who in his allotted time and who before his allotted time.* By the time we came to *Shema Koleinu,* "Hear our voice, Oh Lord, and answer us with mercy and compassion," the very air in the Hut was thick and heavy with the intensity of our prayers and emotions. How could the Almighty not have heard and been moved?

We were relieved a few days later when the holidays of Sukkot and Simchat Torah arrived with their attendant celebrations. Somehow the boys erected a *sukkah* in the space behind the Hut; somehow Rabbi Schonfeld managed to find a *lulav* and *etrog*, the palm branch and citron, which appeared on the eve of the holiday as if by magic; somehow we found and made decorations with which to adorn our *sukkah*; and somehow we were able to throw off the melancholy of Yom Kippur and rejoice.

Bubu committed a cardinal sin while we were in Shefford for which no girl ever forgave him. He had the chutzpah to get married. And whom did he marry? None other than Chumi, the elder sister of my classmate and friend Malka, the very girl who had given me my nickname on the Meadow. Through their successful union, Bubu and Chumi proved that a "mixed marriage" between a boy with a German background, a *Yekke*, and a girl from a Chassidic background, was possible. Not only didn't we forgive Bubu, we also didn't forgive Chumi for capturing him, and we included Malka in our spiteful little vendetta. Poor blameless Malka. It took a while before any girl in the class would speak to her again. Some years after the war, Malka married a young man who turned out to have been one of my father's students in Vienna. (Many years later, Bubu, by then having made aliyah with Chumi and their family, and having somewhere along the way picked up the title of "Rabbi," became financial director of the Laniado Hospital in Netanya, Israel.)

The Hut, which served as our dining room for all meals, was also our social hall. The trestle tables were dismantled and stored at the side of the room, the Ping-Pong table was hauled out, and everyone scrambled to get his or her name on the list to play. One of the older boys, Solly B., who must have been about sixteen, had the loose frame of an athlete and was a fantastic Ping-Pong player. I had a tremendous crush on him. He, of course, was unaware that twelve-year-old girls existed. At other times, the Hut was the theater for our plays and musicals or was used for school assemblies.

In the evenings, after supper, we sat at the tables and did our homework. We received report cards but had no one to show them to, no one who might be proud or disappointed in our progress. What motivated us to study and do well without parental encouragement is a mystery. But motivated we were, and many of us did well. Perhaps we hoped that when we saw our parents again we would be able to show them how hard we had worked despite their absence, or perhaps because of it. Most Sheffordians were high achievers. (Kurt S., the boy who tutored me in math, became a physician, despite the fact that in Shefford we had no laboratory facilities and no classes in chemistry or the other sciences required for acceptance to medical school. I hope Kurt had more success in medicine than he had trying to teach me algebra!) Others became nurses, lawyers, rabbis, cantors, engineers, scientists, teachers, professors, and writers. There were even a couple of politicians in the mix.

* * *

Rabbi Schonfeld still lived in London but visited us in Shefford very often to make sure that everything was running smoothly. He had time for everything and everyone. We children came to him with complaints that were very important to us but must have been inconsequential to him. Yet he always took each of our complaints seriously and tried to solve each problem. One day, I complained to him that my shoes were too small, my toes were becoming infected, and the matron had turned a deaf ear to my request for new shoes. I also needed a new pair of plimsoles for sports and gymnastics.

The matron in charge of clothing, Miss. D., was my nemesis. Just as I had been a favorite of the Cardiff matron, Mrs. Z., I was just the opposite with Miss D. Because I was such a tomboy and went around with my clothes held together by safety pins, Miss D. felt I did not deserve anything new. When parcels of clothing arrived from the charity organizations, she distributed them to girls like Pepi and Marga, "who," she said, "always look nice. Frieda, on the other hand," she added, "always looks like a *schlump* and doesn't deserve any new clothes." When it was time each week to give us our pocket money, Miss D. often searched for an excuse to withhold my shilling. Rabbi Schonfeld, though in the midst of much weightier matters such as finding the finances with which to run his school and continuing his efforts to rescue Jews from Europe, immediately took up my cause as if it were the most important thing on his mind. After making sure that Miss D.

understood that I was entitled to receive my shilling regularly, he gave her money to buy new shoes and plimsoles for me. Perhaps he noticed that I looked like a *schlump*, for he also ordered her to see to it that I received some new blouses and skirts when the next shipment of clothes arrived.

Miss D. was a refugee from Vienna and had been studying law at the time of the *Anschluss*. She was a tall, thin, joyless woman, with pale, nearsighted eyes and a concave chest that made her appear slightly humpbacked. I don't recall ever seeing her smile. She must have been in her midthirties at the time but to us seemed much older. Miss D. resented Rabbi Schonfeld's order to buy me new shoes, yet had no choice but to obey. Annoyance was evident in her every gesture and in the thin line of her rigidly pursed lips as we sat in the train all the way to London and back, without exchanging one word.

We arrived at Oxford Street in silence, and went in silence from one shoe store to another before finding a pair of shoes and a pair of plimsoles that fit me properly and were within the budget Miss D. had been given. After that, she led me into Boots, the chemists, and purchased a purple box with large black printed letters on it, which I vaguely recognized as containing something that the older girls used once a month. She shoved the unwrapped box into my hands, indicating, still wordlessly, that I was to carry it for her. (There was a wartime shortage of paper, and shopkeepers expected customers to bring their own shopping bags.) Still in silence, she had me walk almost the whole length of Oxford Street clutching the exposed and very recognizable purple box in one hand, and the shoe boxes in the other, and then all the way back to Shefford in the train. My embarrassment was so great, I didn't know where to look. I tried to hide the offensive box behind the shoe boxes, but to no avail; it slipped out of my hand, causing Miss D. to cluck impatiently while I scrambled awkwardly to pick it up. She made no effort to help me. Pedestrians passed us and snickered behind their hands when they noticed the box I was carrying. I wished a snap of my fingers would make me invisible. Luckily we had the train compartment to ourselves on the return journey, but for the whole ride I worried that some boys might see me carrying the box before I could get rid of it. By the time we arrived at the White House, I was a nervous wreck. I was relieved that no one was around, and before we entered I shoved the offensive box into Miss D.'s hands and ran inside without waiting for her to protest.

Food rationing was severe, and Miss D. held all our ration cards. While margarine was still plentiful, butter was strictly rationed and doled out just twice a week for breakfast on a slice of white bread. Rumor had it that Miss D. held back eggs and butter and other rationed items, which she then shared with her favorites, some of the older girls with whom she was apparently on good terms. I was in the enviable position of hating the taste of butter or milk. (I was probably what is known today as "lactose intolerant," though that condition was not recognized at the time.) On "butter days," I arrived for breakfast at the White House to find a queue of supplicants waiting to request my butter bread and my shredded wheat with milk. Not being a fool, I haggled and bartered. With Annette, for instance, I negotiated an easy exchange, because she was a vegetarian and was only too happy to barter her meat ration (two slices one night a week for supper) for my butter bread. Walter, who wanted my shredded wheat with milk, had nothing of value to exchange in the way of food that appealed to me, so here the negotiations became a bit trickier. In the end I settled for a book, a collection of Shakespeare plays. I still believe I got the better of the bargain. My breakfast usually consisted of bread and margarine and, occasionally, as a special treat, scrambled eggs made from egg powder. Thursday nights, we invariably had fried cod or hake with mashed potatoes for supper, one of my favorite meals, even though the fish was swimming in oil. I always tried to get my turn at kitchen duty on Thursday nights so as to receive an extra helping of fried fish.

Trudy R. was our nurse, a refugee like us. She took care of our cuts and scrapes and bruises and, most important, treated us when we had lice. She occupied a small room, the surgery, on the top floor of the White House, where she carried out her ministrations. The first time I found a louse crawling on my comb I turned to Edith, who had already experienced a delousing, and asked her, "Doesn't everyone have a few?"

Trudy made sure we went for regular dental checkups to a Jewish dentist in Letchworth, who treated us without charge. When a serious medical emergency arose, the village doctor was called in. Fortunately, during the time I was in Shefford I never needed his attention. We all loved Trudy, who was kind and gentle and always ready to comfort the younger children when they came crying to her in pain. I have a very clear memory of Trudy holding a little girl on her lap. The child was crying, either from some minor hurt or simply from unhappiness. She must have been about six or seven, the age I was when I arrived in England. The sight tugged at my heart and I felt a lump rise in my throat. I turned away, not realizing then that what I was feeling was jealousy in its rawest form. The memory of Mimi taking me on her lap seemed to have happened to someone else, or in one of my dreams, a long, long time before.

Trudy also explained to us girls what the "curse" was all about and what to do when it occurred, and it was from her that I found out, to my chagrin, that this was not something experienced only by *shiksas*.

On the same floor as the surgery was the welfare room, in which stood a solitary old sewing machine. Miss D. had a constant stream of volunteer ladies working on that machine, repairing our torn clothes. Other ladies darned socks and sewed by hand. We were expected to wash our own dirty laundry, and Trudy showed us how to first soak our underwear in cold water before using hot water and soap to remove stains.

Edith and I washed our few clothes at our billet and, when the weather allowed, hung them up with wooden clothes pegs to dry on a clothesline in the garden, or on a line strung across our attic room when it was raining or snowing. Our landlady, Mrs. L., was a world-weary, dour, unsmiling woman, whose days revolved around her husband and two children. I have but a shadowy memory of her, for we rarely saw her except to mutter a greeting when we came and went, and we had no sustained conversations with her that I recall. She and her husband had been uprooted from their comfortable life in Frankfurt or Leipzig or Berlin, or whichever German city they had lived in before the war. In their previous existence they had been important members of a thriving Jewish community. Overnight, they found themselves in a strange little country village in a foreign land, surrounded by gentile neighbors who did not speak their language. But at least they had escaped with their family intact. My recollection of Mr. L. also remains elusive, for he left the house very early each morning to catch the London train. What he did in London I never found out, nor did I learn how he had made a living in Germany before the war. The daughter had already graduated from Rabbi Schonfeld's school and had a job in Letchworth; the son, a studious, clever boy, was in one of the upper forms and was also soon to graduate.

Edith and I rarely crossed paths with either the daughter or the son, for they slept on the second floor of the house, while Edith and I shared the attic right under the roof. The attic had sharply sloping, bare-beamed ceilings, and we had to be very careful getting out of bed and walking around the room so as not to hit our heads and fill our hands and faces with wood splinters, which of course we did over and over again. Next to the attic, separated by a wooden partition, was a small storage space in which Mrs. L. stored barrels of apples in winter. The cold under the roof preserved the apples for months on end. Whenever Edith and I thought we could get away with it, we gave in to the temptation to appropriate an apple or two. If Mrs. L. noticed her stock of Coxes' Orange Pippins depleting, she never mentioned it.

I suppose Mrs. Thorndike had it right: I was nothing but a little Jewish thief.

A mumps epidemic was sweeping through the school like wildfire. My friend Sonja, a pretty, somewhat overweight girl from Frankfurt, told me she thought she was coming down with it; the glands around her neck felt swollen. Sonja and her two younger sisters, Zelma and Gala, had escaped from Europe with their parents just before the war started. Tragically, their mother passed away shortly after they arrived in London, and their father, unable to care for three young girls on his own, sent them to Shefford. Sonja's news thrilled me. I was very anxious to contract mumps in order to avoid taking the final exams that were due to start the following week. I rubbed my face against hers and asked her to breathe into my mouth, desperately hoping that I would catch her germs. No such luck. Sonja came down with a bad case of mumps a couple of days later. I stayed healthy and had to do some serious last-minute swotting before sitting for final exams.

One day we were called to a special assembly at which Bubu made an exciting announcement. "Boys and girls, we are getting a very important visitor from London, none other than Sir Adrian Boult, the famous conductor." Somehow Bubu had met Sir Adrian in London and had aroused the famous conductor's humanitarian interest and curiosity about the unusual school of Jewish refugees tucked away in a little English village. Because of Bubu, we were familiar with the names of many orchestra conductors, and when we heard the news we all went into a dither of activity, running here and there to spruce up the White House and make ourselves presentable. Bubu said he had received permission from the vicar of St. Michael's Church to borrow the church hall in which to welcome our illustrious visitor.

Bubu rehearsed our choir relentlessly for hours and hours on end, until we could have sung the songs in our sleep. The day of Sir Adrian's visit arrived. All the members of the choir stood waiting nervously on the stage. We girls were instructed to wear white blouses and dark skirts, the boys white shirts and black trousers. All the boys owned white shirts and black trousers because that is what they wore on Shabbat, but there were not enough white blouses to go around for all the girls. As a result, all the white blouses stood in the front row of the choir and the rest of us tried to be unobtrusive in our colored blouses at the back. The whole village of Shefford and the surrounding villages had been invited, and the hall was packed to capacity

The Queen entered together with Sir Adrian, a bald, handsome man with a regal bearing and a thick salt-and-pepper mustache. The two of them made an imposing couple. Bubu lifted his baton and we were off. We sang the round "*Shalom Aleichem*" for our guest, except instead of the Hebrew words we substituted Latin. *Dona nobis pacem*, Give us peace. The echoes of that glorious day remain with me, and I can still hear our voices as they tore into the rafters of the church hall and rattled the stained glass windows. I'm sure Sir Adrian was suitably impressed. He invited us all to see him conduct at the Royal Albert Hall after the war was over. Many of us asked him for his autograph and he graciously obliged.

*　*　*

I no longer dreamed of my parents or Oma. Before going to sleep I tried to conjure up their faces, hoping I would dream of them, but I couldn't remember what they looked like, and I had no photographs. Every night, after saying the Shema, I prayed to God: *Dear God, I will not talk anymore during* davening; *I will stand all day on Yom Kippur; I will try not to crib on my geometry test, if you will only bring Mama and Papa back to us.*

By the spring of 1945 it was clear that the Nazis were on the run and that it was just a matter of weeks before the war would be over, at least in Europe. I couldn't help thinking about the Whyte-Smiths and imagining how happy the Colonel must be now that his maps had to be covered with blue pins. I felt very ambivalent at the thought of leaving Shefford, even though I was looking forward with great anticipation, as I imagine we all were, to what lay in store for us in London and – dare we think about it? – to being reunited with our parents. Shefford was the place where, for the first time since I left Vienna, I felt safe. It was the place where I did not feel utterly powerless; where I was able to express myself; where I was able to achieve recognition through study and sports; where I felt valued by friends and teachers; where I was not looked down upon because I was a refugee. Shefford was the place where, for the first time in my life, I did not experience any anti-Semitism. It was the place where my religious observance matured, took root, and flourished, and where the Jewish path that I would follow for the rest of my life, with only a little falter here and there, was laid out for me.

It was also the place where I made so many lifelong friends.

On May 8, 1945, VE day was declared – Victory in Europe. The war was finally over. In Shefford, naturally, we celebrated together with the rest of the country. The whole village turned out; there was dancing in the streets with music blaring from loudspeakers, banners and streamers strung all over the place, and the Union Jack hanging from every window. All the windows were stripped of their blackout coverings, and at night Old Bridge Street was lit up as we had never seen it before.

Inside the White House, our jubilation was somewhat more subdued. Now we expected to hear the fate of our parents. By now we had learned about the concentration camps, mostly from newsreels that showed their liberation and the unspeakable acts of cruelty and inhumanity that our people had suffered at the hands of the Nazi butchers. We watched the screen in speechless horror and forced ourselves not to look away from the skeletal survivors whose eyes stared out sightlessly, without expression, from hollow orbs. We gazed unbelieving and sick to our stomachs at the mounds and mounds of dead bodies, thrown like rag dolls one on top of the other, and silently wondered, *Could that be my father; is that my mother? Could that corpse be my grandmother?*

Six million. The number was impossible to comprehend, to absorb. I began having nightmares again. My dreams were filled with barbed wire, skeletal corpses, chimneys belching black smoke, menacing shadowy figures wearing swastikas, snarling dogs chasing me. In these dreams I was always running, running, trying to escape, and I would wake up in the middle of the night in a pool of sweat, panting as if I had really been running, and unable for several moments to get my bearings.

On our last morning in Shefford, we milled around outside the White House, rucksacks strapped to our backs, waiting for the buses that were to transport us to our new lives in London. There was a lot of laughter and excitement overshadowing the touch of sadness we felt at the prospect of leaving this village where we had been so happy and safe. We wandered around the White House, saying goodbye to each room: the Hut, the Queen's office, the surgery, and trying to memorize them forever. Many of the villagers came to see us off, and there were a lot of tears and emotional farewells, especially on the part of some of the village women who had lost husbands or sons in the war. Promises were made to write and stay in touch. Indeed, many children stayed in touch with their gentile foster parents for many years after the war, sent them Christmas cards and presents when they could, and even went back to Shefford to visit them from time to time. Our presence in the village had brought a new dimension into their lives, and many of the villagers were sorry to see us go.

While waiting for the buses, we exchanged messages with each other in our autograph books. My friends and classmates all received the same message from me: *Never forget the last hour in Shefford.*

CHAPTER SIX

LONDON

In London our buses took us to an old bomb-damaged mansion, which Rabbi Schonfeld had found for us on Woodbury Down, near Finsbury Park. Miss D. had gone ahead with Trudy and other helpers to ready our new home. Miss D. was to be the matron of the hostel. In this leaky old house, so poorly heated that in winter we developed festering, debilitating chilblains on our hands and feet, we waited for news of our parents. In my daydreams I sometimes imagined that they had reached Palestine but were unable for some reason to locate us; at other times I was convinced that they had escaped to Siberia, where they were so isolated that they didn't know the war had ended. Another fantasy had them suffering from amnesia, wandering around helplessly, unable to remember even their own names, let alone their children. In bed at night, after saying the Shema, I sometimes asked God, "Is this my punishment for eating *treif*, for desecrating Shabbat?"

He never answered.

While we waited, we attended Rabbi Schonfeld's school – renamed Avigdor High School in memory of the rabbi's father – on

Lordship Road. Dr. Judith Grunfeld, the Queen, still reigned as our headmistress. I was happy and proud to be named Girls' Sports Captain, and also received the dubious distinction of being appointed prefect, as a result of which my popularity with the younger children automatically plummeted to zero!

I shared a room with Pepi, Marga, Sonja, and two older girls: Gypsy, who was also from Vienna, and Dora, a girl from Danzig. Gypsy, whose real name was Bertha, had earned her nickname in Shefford because of her fiery disposition, flashing black eyes, and love of dancing. Dora was a happy-go-lucky, tousle-headed girl with a beautiful voice that could be heard trilling from morning to night throughout the hostel. She sang songs from the Jeannette MacDonald–Nelson Eddy pictures, which she never tired of seeing over and over again. We often teased her about the "Indian Love Song." She sang "When I'm calling you-ooh-ooh-ooh, ooh-ooh-ooh…," and we mimicked her repeatedly in the last bars, but she took it good-naturedly. Dora had finished high school and was learning a trade with a promising future: she was being trained to touch up black-and-white pictures with color. My old friend Edith found an uncle in California who had survived the war; he sent her papers and she left for America.

In our free time we explored a crippled but unbowed London, discovering its museums, galleries, theaters, and concert halls. Art collections were just beginning to be returned to the British Museum, the Tate, and the other museums where they belonged. The collections, like us, had been evacuated to country destinations at the start of the war, and they had been hidden in secret locations. The Tate was the first museum that most of us had ever visited and we couldn't get enough of it. We were frequent visitors to the Royal Albert Hall, also a "first," since none of us had ever attended a live concert before. I particularly remember one concert that Bubu put on at the Royal Albert Hall when he was wearing his impresario hat: Beethoven's Ninth, the *Choral Symphony*, conducted by none other than Sir Adrian Boult, whom we had first met when he visited us in Shefford. I had heard that people complained that the acoustics in the Royal Albert Hall were not very good, but to my untrained ear that concert with its resounding chorale finale was a *pièce de résistance*. On another occasion we attended a performance of Handel's *Messiah*, also conducted by Sir Adrian. Once again, the singing was magnificent and our enthusiastic applause brought Sir Adrian back onto the stage over and over again for more bows and encores.

The scaffolds that had been erected to protect some of the historical monuments were being dismantled, and blackout coverings all over the city were torn down. The Houses of Parliament and Big Ben, the Tower of London, Trafalgar and Piccadilly Squares, were once again ablaze with light. We took boat rides through the locks of the Thames to Hampton Court and Windsor, and went on Lag B'Omer outings to Dorking and Margate. We saw our first live musical, *Annie Get Your Gun*, at a theater in the West End; we saw Shakespeare's *Hamlet*, starring Laurence Olivier, at the Old Vic, and Michael Redgrave in *Macbeth*; we heard our first live opera, *La Bohème*, at Covent Garden (still in scaffolds because of bomb damage), and were introduced to Sadler's Wells Royal Ballet, where Margot Fonteyn reigned as prima ballerina. Closer to home, we explored the ruins of houses on Woodbury Down that had been completely demolished in the Blitz, all the while totally ignorant and heedless of the unexploded bombs and rats that undoubtedly lurked beneath the rubble.

In August we learned about the atomic bombs that were dropped on Hiroshima and Nagasaki. On the fifteenth of the month the Japanese surrendered and vj Day was declared. Victory over Japan. We saw pictures in the newspapers of the mushroom clouds and watched the newsreels with a kind of horrified fascination. But the events in the Pacific were too remote to be of more than passing interest or to register deeply, too far away to affect us; they were but a distant addendum to the defeat of the Nazis in Europe. Our concerns were more immediate. We were still trying to trace the fate of our parents and adjusting to our new lives in London. We could not concern ourselves too much with events taking place on the other side of the world.

*   *   *

We continued putting on our Purim and Chanukah *spiels*, which satirized and parodied Miss D., our teachers and each other. No one was spared. Two brothers, Saly and Jacob F., were clever and witty writers of skits and jokes. Sometimes, however, they were guilty of blurring the line between humor and insensitivity. For instance, one of the younger boys, David S., regularly wet his bed. In the Chanukah show we put on that first year after our return to London, the riddle was posed: What is the difference between David S. and a sailor? The answer: A sailor makes his bed on the ocean, David makes an ocean in his bed. Even though I laughed along with everyone, in my heart I squirmed with discomfort. Because of my own past experience in the bed-wetting department, I couldn't help feeling that David must have been terribly mortified. (The two brothers eventually made aliyah and Jacob subsequently became a reporter for the *Jerusalem Post*).

On Shabbat mornings we attended Rabbi Schonfeld's shul in Green Lanes, the Adas Yisroel. Under his tallit, Rabbi Schonfeld always wore pin-striped tails and a top hat, all very British. We girls sat in the women's gallery upstairs and didn't *daven* very much; we were at the age when we liked to watch the boys below and nudged each other when we thought the object of that week's affection was looking up at us. Rabbi Schonfeld was a dynamic speaker and still had that unusual timbre in his voice that I remembered so well from the first time we met; it was impossible not to pay attention during his *drashot*. After services he always stood outside and greeted each of us by name, asking something personal and wanting to know how we were getting on. I believe it was on one of these occasions that I reported to him that Miss D. had once again confiscated my pocket money, this time because I had made a sloppy hospital corner on my bed. He didn't seem to mind being bothered with such a trivial matter, and on Shabbat to boot. I thought he would forget about the whole thing, but of course, he didn't. He was actually quite outraged and I heard that he gave Miss D. a dressing down, which did nothing to endear me to her.

Some time in the 1950s Miss D. married and moved to Australia. She assumed her husband's Germanic name, one that had a certain ironic ring to it: *Kinderlehrer.* Translated, it means "teacher of children."

Intellectually, I know I should forgive Miss D.; who knows what hardships the poor woman suffered, how many loved ones she left behind or lost in Vienna? Emotionally, though, it is not so easy. Several years after my marriage I received a phone call from Ruth S., one of the older Sheffordians. Miss D. and her husband were coming to New York on a visit. Would I be interested in attending a reception for them? Ruth obviously knew nothing of my checkered history with Miss D., and she must have been quite startled when I laughed into the phone, and even more startled by my churlish and adamant refusal of her invitation.

It is many years now since I learned that Miss D. passed away. In the interim my soul has soldiered on in a state of limbo: not quite forgiving, not quite able to absolve her. I think of Miss D. each Yom Kippur when I search my soul and pound my breast in remorse for all my many sins, and wonder, not without some regret, at the lasting effect she seems to have had on me. But I'm happy to report that each Yom Kippur my heart inches closer and closer to total forgiveness.

And yet....

On long, lazy Shabbat afternoons in the summer months, when stars often did not make their appearance before ten thirty at night, a group of us usually walked over to Clissold Park. Long before we reached the park, we could hear strains of music coming from the bandstand, that unique and ubiquitous British institution born in the reign of Queen Victoria. The park was bursting with throngs of people enjoying the free concerts that, for many, were their only form of entertainment in a dreary post-war week of continued food rationing, crowded bomb-damaged housing, and sacrifice. The crowds reacted to the music like thirsty, weary travelers who have miraculously stumbled upon an oasis in the middle of the Sahara.

We girls strolled nonchalantly, arm in arm, on the path that snaked around the bandstand, pretending that the purpose of our visit to the park was purely cultural, to listen to the music blaring from the brass band. Of course, while we promenaded we pretended to ignore the hostel boys standing on the sidelines among the noisy spectators. All the while, from the corner of our eyes, we secretly observed the boys to see if they were paying attention to what we were wearing, to the way we were walking and talking and laughing, all of which we hoped showed us off to maximum advantage.

Often our broken-down hostel had no hot water and we were unable to bathe. When that happened, we were given money and sent to the public baths on Mare Street in Hackney. How I loved those outings to the public baths! As soon as I entered, I was immediately assaulted by the warm steamy air, which I sniffed and breathed in contentedly. An attendant handed me a towel and showed me to my cubicle where hot water was already pouring into the bath. Each cubicle was numbered, and so for the next half hour we could be heard yelling, "More hot water in number fourteen please!"; "Soap in number seven please!"; "A towel in number two please!" We shouted nonsense to each other over the cubicle partitions and laughed with sheer happiness, until the attendant begged us to keep it down. What a treat it was for us to luxuriate in a hot bath, something we were never able to do in the hostel, where the hot water was forever running out and there was always someone pounding on the bathroom door and yelling, "Hurry up, for heaven's sake, don't you know other people need to wash?" I'd stay in that public bath until the last possible moment, until my fingers were shriveled like an ancient crone's and my skin tingled and glowed from the heat and from the unaccustomed scrubbing.

* * *

In November 1946 we welcomed more of Rabbi Schonfeld's "children": those he rescued after the war from Poland and Czechoslovakia, children who had been placed for safekeeping by their parents in convents and monasteries, or who had survived by hiding in caves and forests. It was very dangerous for Rabbi Schonfeld to travel to Eastern Europe on these rescue missions. Many of the Polish families who sheltered Jewish children had become attached to them and were loath to surrender them. On one occasion a disgruntled anti-Semitic Pole actually took a shot at him. Fortunately, he missed. After that incident, the British government issued Rabbi Schonfeld a major's uniform, in the hope that this official and visible military rank would protect him from similar attacks.

We old-timers referred to the newcomers as "the Polish children." Some of them were wild and unmanageable because of their wartime experiences. Many of them suffered from nightmares and were often found sleepwalking. One boy was a kleptomaniac; he was discovered stealing money from the charity boxes. Another boy insisted on sleeping with a knife under his pillow. (He later became a surgeon!) Some of the children would lean over their plates possessively when eating and not raise their heads until their plates were licked clean, afraid someone might snatch the food from under their noses before they could finish.

One lovely Polish girl, Fela, became my close friend. I believe ours was the only lasting friendship forged in the hostel that crossed the line between the Polish and "English" children. Fela had been a small child in the Warsaw Ghetto and was thrown over the ghetto wall in a daring and dangerous escape. Afterward, during her years of hiding with a gentile family in the Polish countryside, she suffered an appendicitis attack and had her appendix removed in an emergency operation on a kitchen table. Many years later, after Fela married, it was discovered that she could not bear children as a result of that primitive procedure. Fela's mother and little sister also survived in Poland; her mother sent the two girls to England with Rabbi Schonfeld on one of his postwar rescue missions and later followed them as a domestic, the only way she was able to enter the country.

I was happy when Miss D. reorganized our sleeping arrangements and I found myself in a smaller room with Fela and one other girl, Hedy. Miss D. may have wanted to separate me from my old Shefford crowd as some form of punishment, but the move had quite the opposite effect. Hedy, too, had arrived in the hostel in 1946, after having been hidden in a convent in Belgium for the last two years of the war. Hedy was a beautiful girl but a little on the plump side. She had a crush on Joe, a redhead, who habitually taunted her about her weight. Hoping to make her feel better, I told her that Joe must obviously like her or he wouldn't bother to tease her. The next time he teased her, I heard Hedy tell him, "I know you must like me or you wouldn't call me names. Frieda said so!"

Fela had, and still has, the greatest sense of humor and an irresistible, infectious laugh. From Fela I learned to laugh as I had never laughed before. I even learned to laugh about Miss D. and found that the *Readers' Digest* was right: laughter *is* the best medicine. I was amazed that after her experiences in the Warsaw Ghetto and later, hiding out with Polish gentiles, in daily fear of being discovered by the Nazis, Fela was able to laugh at all. (Today, when we get together we just have to look at each other and burst out laughing for no reason at all. A couple of years ago, Fela and her husband visited us from their home in Toronto, and I organized a dinner party in their honor. When Fela admired the floral arrangement and the way I had set the table, I told her I had learned this art in the hostel. We both collapsed with laughter and were still laughing when the other guests arrived.)

Our feelings toward the Polish children were somewhat ambivalent. On the one hand, we regarded ourselves as "British" by now and felt superior to these foreigners who spoke an ugly, guttural language. Their arrival upset the equilibrium and routine of our lives, causing tensions and resentment. We were displaced from one of the downstairs rooms that had been our common room and contained the Ping-Pong table; it was converted into a dormitory for some of the Polish boys. As a result, we were now unable to play Ping-Pong. The newcomers had no hesitation about speaking Polish in our presence, and often we felt they were talking about us and laughing at our expense. On the other hand, we knew we should feel compassion for the Polish children. They had really suffered; they had not sat out the war years in the safety of the British countryside as we had. They had been in the direct line of fire; their lives had been in constant danger. They were the real refugees, the true survivors.

Often, on Sunday evenings, the Polish children would commandeer the homework room, move the tables to the wall, and set up their gramophone. The Polish girls would dance to the popular tunes of the day and to old standards such as Strauss waltzes. We "English" children watched with a kind of disapproving fascination as the girls danced and twirled and dipped with abandon and glided gracefully with their partners around the room. The Polish boys, too, looked on, laughing and joking and kibitzing with each other in a language that was as foreign to us as the girls' performances. I dimly recalled the Howells in Staines and the way they had pulled back the carpet and danced with each other, but in Cardiff and Shefford, and until now in the hostel, our only dance had been the *horah*. There was something deliciously wicked in this spectacle that filled us "English" children with a wistful, almost guilty feeling, as if we were taking part in forbidden fruit, even though all we did was watch.

Later, in the privacy of our room, Fela tried to teach me the fox-trot. Alas, her efforts were in vain. We discovered to my dismay, but amidst a lot of laughter, that I was still in possession of two left feet. (It was not until many years later that I learned from Fela that the Polish children, rather than referring to us among themselves as the "English children," as we had assumed, had labeled us "the *German* children.")

The Polish children also caused an upheaval in our religious life; most of them did not come from observant homes. Many of them had spent the war years in convents and monasteries where they had lived as Catholics. They knew more about Catholicism than they did about Judaism and, at first, some of them tended to mock our practices.

Eventually, though, the Polish children became integrated; they learned the language quickly, and their wartime paranoia subsided. Many of them became observant as a result of the training they received in Rabbi Schonfeld's school and in our hostel. I recall one humorous incident that occurred soon after their arrival, when the language must still have been very new to them. One of the boys called a cinema, which was playing a film they wanted to see, and in broken English asked for directions how to get there. The lady at the other end of the line asked, "Where are you coming from?" The boy answered, "From Poland." To which the lady responded, "In that case you'd better take a plane!"

*   *   *

Now that we were in London and I had my married sisters living not too far away, I was no longer quite so intimidated by Miss D. Nor was I so dependent on her whims regarding clothing, because every now and then, when Miriam could afford it, she would buy me something, or pass down one of her old suits. In fact, from Fela I learned to handle the situation with humor. "I have one blouse for every day of the week," I was fond of telling my friends, "and this is it!" The Polish children weren't in awe of Miss D., and their attitude also helped to neutralize the effect she had on me. As a matter of fact, the Polish children didn't seem to be in awe of anyone; their wartime experiences, I imagine, had given them a jaundiced view of those in positions of authority. They were able to handle Miss D. with humor. When she retired to her office each Thursday evening to work on her accounts, she hung a sign on her door to indicate that she should not be disturbed. The sign read *Engaged*. Invariably, one of the Polish boys would scribble underneath, "*Mazal Tov!*"

Some of the tricks the Polish boys played on each other were not so humorous. For inventiveness and ingenuity, however, the tricks they cooked up deserved some kind of an award – for cruelty if nothing else.

The incident I remember best concerned Henyek, a young Polish boy of about thirteen or fourteen. Henyek was a timid, nervous boy and, unlike some of the other boys, had come out of the war afraid of his own shadow. Certainly he needed some tender loving care and should never have been placed in the downstairs dormitory among the older, tougher Polish boys. What the boys did was quite incredible. They told Henyek that the hostel was not really a home for children but that it was a cover for something much more sinister. The hostel, they told him, was really a lunatic asylum!

When Henyek expressed disbelief, the boys claimed to have broken into Miss D.'s office and stolen her records. (Prior to this incident, the boys had approached each of us asking for a recent photograph. We girls were so flattered that naturally we handed our photographs over without questioning the purpose.) They showed Henyek a book they had craftily compiled, listing the name and photograph of each child with a comment next to each name giving a diagnosis. There were triangles next to each child's name; the number of triangles denoted the severity of each particular case. One triangle meant that the child was not severely damaged and might respond to treatment; two triangles indicated a more serious condition, while three triangles meant that there was little hope for a cure. They showed Henyek the page listing his name, next to which, of course, appeared three triangles.

Henyek was not quite as gullible as the boys thought; he knew their reputation for playing tricks, and even after being shown Miss D.'s "book," he did not immediately swallow the story. But the boys were ready for him. For several consecutive nights, Henyek was awakened after midnight by one of the boys and made to watch a different scene unfold. On one night the boy who slept with a knife under his pillow was seen straddling a chair next to the open window with the moonlight shining into his eyes while he sharpened his knife on a leather strop with deliberate, frenzied motions, all the while glaring into the distance with a maniacal look in his eyes. When Henyek tried to speak to him, he received no answer; the boy pretended to be acting in his sleep, unable to hear a thing. The following night Henyek was again awakened, this time to the sight of another boy, a mathematical genius, striding back and forth across the room pretending to be a sleepwalking Pythagoras declaiming various theorems in a wild and frightening manner. On the third night, Henyek was awakened yet again. This time he was led to the window, where he saw one of the boys, a good athlete, climbing up a drainpipe onto the roof of the hostel. There was a full moon that night, and the sight of the boy's dark silhouette against the moon, teetering precariously on the gutter's edge, caused Henyek to moan with fright and disbelief. This kind of thing went on for several nights, until Henyek became a total bundle of nerves, unable and afraid to fall asleep. Finally he ran to Miss D.'s office and pounded on the door, crying hysterically. As soon as Miss D. opened the door, Henyek fell to his knees, clutched at her dress, mumbling incoherently through his tears. Miss D. recoiled in horror, but the harder she tried to dislodge Henyek's hands from the hem of her dress, the harder he held on.

Finally he managed to get some words out and beseeched her, "Miss D., Miss D., I beg you. Please take one triangle away from my name, please, just one triangle, that's all I ask!"

I don't recall what happened to Henyek after that. I know he was transferred to another bedroom upstairs where some of the younger boys slept. Whether the tricksters suffered any consequences, or even any pangs of conscience, is doubtful. I certainly saw no signs of remorse. To the contrary, they seemed very pleased with the way their prank had worked and congratulated themselves on their ingenuity. That poor little Henyek didn't land in a real asylum was a miracle. Some years later he made aliyah and I lost sight of him.

* * *

A group of British do-gooders, young men and women in their twenties and thirties, obviously well heeled, decided to adopt the hostel as their pet charity. On Sundays and holidays they would come around, talk and spend time with us, and sometimes take us on picnic outings or to the theater. A few weeks before Chanukah we were told to write down what we wanted as a Chanukah present and, if it was within reason, the committee would try to get it for us. To this day I can't explain why I was unable to bring myself to write down my request. I had just learned to ice-skate and badly wanted a pair of skates. But just as I had been unable to bring the word *Aunty* past my lips when calling for Mrs. Simmons, and just as I was unable to tell Mrs. Whyte-Smith that what I most wanted for Christmas was a bicycle, so was I unable to get my hand to write the words *ice skates*. All of the other children's requests were granted; Dora had asked for ice skates and received a beautiful white leather pair with shiny blades. Because the committee had received no request from me, they had not known what to get me. As a result, I received an orange jumper, which I detested; it was too tight, anyway. I tossed it into my drawer and never wore it.

In late 1947 Princess Elizabeth married Philip Mountbatten, who was subsequently named Duke of Edinburgh. The day of the wedding was declared a national holiday and all the cinemas were open free of charge and showed the ceremony in Westminster Abbey at simultaneous screenings. My friends and I managed to get into the Astoria Cinema, the very same one to which the Simmonses had taken me on that fateful Shabbat soon after my arrival in London. The inside was still adorned exactly as I remembered it. The wedding ceremony of the pretty princess and her Prince Charming was a fairy tale come true, and all of us watched the royal processions, the glittering chariots, the church service, and all the pomp and circumstance, with open-mouthed wonder.

A few months after the arrival of the Polish children, I realized I was being followed, and by none other than M., the boy who slept with a knife under his pillow! Apparently M. had developed a crush on me and, now that he could speak a little English, kept trying to engage me in conversation. I was petrified. I asked Fela and Hedy and the other girls to make sure I was never left alone with him, and whenever I was walking with the girls and he came into view, I begged them not to leave me. M., on the other hand, lingered and dawdled behind me even when he was with some of the other Polish boys. He made every effort to pry me away from the other girls and get me to walk with him. By now I had picked up a couple of words of Polish and, when his friends tried to get him to walk on, I heard him tell them, "*Czekaj, czekaj chwile* [Wait, wait a moment]."

Sometime in 1948 M. and another Polish boy volunteered to go off and fight the Arabs in the newly founded State of Israel. Somehow M. managed to corner me alone one evening in the garden. He begged me not to run away before hearing what he had to say. I was shaking with fright. There was no one in sight and I was frightened that he would try to touch me, perhaps even try to kiss me. However he behaved like a gentleman. He told me in fairly fluent English that he was going to Israel to fight the Arabs, perhaps to be killed, but that he loved me and begged me to write to him. I don't remember what I said. As soon as I could, I escaped and ran into the house. I received several letters from M. They were filled with his imagined love for me. I knew I had to put a stop to them. I wrote back telling him that I was too young for this kind of thing and our relationship had no future. The letters stopped. M. survived, found an uncle in Switzerland who offered to put him through school. Eventually he became a successful physician. He never married.

Just before my sixteenth birthday I received a letter from the British Home Office inviting me to become a British citizen. Because of my *Kindertransport* status, the government was waiving its usual requirements for citizenship. I was very excited. On the appointed day, I dressed carefully in a clean blouse and skirt and took the Tube to the Home Office located near Pall Mall. My heart was pounding as I was shown into an office where a very stern, official-looking elderly gentleman with a white mustache sat behind an imposing desk. He immediately reminded me of Colonel Whyte-Smith.

"So, Miss Stolzberg," he said in the clipped, upper-class inflection of a British civil servant, "I understand you want to become a loyal subject of the British Crown. Eh, what?" This was the first time anyone had ever called me Miss Stolzberg and I became so flustered I hardly knew what to answer. I must have mumbled something though, and before I knew it the gentleman had taken out a large rubber stamp, banged it down on a document on his desk, and held out his hand for me to shake. And that was all there was to it: a bit of letdown, somewhat anti-climactic, and with none of the pomp and circumstance I had expected. I was very proud when my naturalization certificate arrived by post, and I immediately applied for a British passport. I have it still, a dark blue book with a gold crown embossed in the center of the cover, although it has long since expired.

Mrs. Klein encouraged me to attend university after high school. I had done well in English on the national exams; in fact, I was the only one in my form and the first one in the school to receive a "Distinction," the highest mark possible. (On the other hand, my marks in math didn't bear mentioning.) However I needed to earn a living and so, to Mrs. Klein's deep disappointment and my own, after graduation I attended a polytechnic school to learn shorthand, typing, and bookkeeping, skills I needed in order to support myself. I landed my first job with a large insurance company on Fleet Street in the City at the same time that Fela, who had acquired similar skills, got her first job. Because we were now working, we had to move out of the hostel, and Rabbi Schonfeld found a kosher boarding house for us in Hackney, where Fela and I shared a room for over a year.

The boarding house was a three-story affair owned and run by a refugee couple from Poland, Mr. and Mrs. K., and their two sons. Besides Fela and me, there were seven other boarders, all single Jewish boys in their late teens or early twenties. With the two K. sons, that made nine single boys for Fela and me to flirt with! And flirt we did at every opportunity. We were young and carefree and knew nothing serious would result. It was all a lot of innocent but exhilarating fun.

Mrs. K. was an excellent cook and her menus were a welcome change from hostel fare. Every day she packed up sandwiches for us to take to work. Neither of us liked cheese sandwiches, but we didn't want to hurt Mrs. K's feelings by telling her; when she wasn't looking we tossed the sandwiches in the rubbish bin in the back garden. Which was pretty stupid of us, for one day Mrs. K. discovered them and was much more insulted than if we had told her we didn't like cheese sandwiches in the first place. The waste of good food, especially at a time of postwar austerity, was particularly offensive to her. We bought her a little gift to smooth her ruffled feelings, and after that enjoyed getting her delicious salami and egg sandwiches.

Often I spent Shabbat with my sister Miriam, who by then had been married for several years but was still childless. She and her husband lived in a small attached house near Stamford Hill. I knew that my visits and the occasional visits from Ephraim, who was still in yeshiva, were happy interludes in her increasingly oppressive marriage, and so I continued going, even though the presence of her fanatical husband always put a damper on the occasion. The man ruled my sister with an iron fist and her barrenness was an added irritant in their relationship for, in his view, their childlessness could not possibly be laid at his door. He attempted to include me in his tyranny, but I would have none of it. He was opinionated to the point of never being wrong about anything. Once, when I was ill with a stubborn case of bronchitis, he knew better than the doctors: he insisted that I needed leeches placed on my body to suck out the poison and became very angry when I resisted. After I recovered, I determined to stay away from him as much as possible.

I found myself filled with restlessness, wanderlust, and the Zionistic fervor that I had inhaled in Shefford. We still had received no word about the fate of our parents. All our inquiries through the Red Cross met a dead end. Our parents had reached Yugoslavia and then vanished into thin air without a trace. I also felt the need to put distance between myself and my increasingly fanatical and domineering brother-in-law, even though it meant deserting my sister. I decided to make aliyah to the newly founded State of Israel. Many older Sheffordians like Dora and Gypsy had gone ahead of me; some had even fought in the War of Independence. Solly B., the boy on whom I had had a crush in Shefford, had been killed. The Jewish Agency was willing to pay for my passage. In order to accumulate some spending money, and against my better judgment, I moved into my sister's house a few weeks before I was due to leave. I tried to keep the news of my impending departure from my brother-in-law, but of course he found out.

The scene he created is almost indescribable. As a vocal member of the Neturei Karta, he was violently opposed to the new Jewish state. In fact, when the State of Israel was founded, he and his cronies took out advertisements in the London papers cynically inviting King Abdullah of Jordan to become king of Israel! He burst into my bedroom when I was packing, without knocking, foaming at the mouth, so red in the face that I thought he would burst a blood vessel. He was trembling with fury, unable to contain his rage. He came at me, his hands balled up into fists, and I thought he was going to kill me. As frightened as I was, I managed to stand my ground and faced him down, taunting him, "Come on, *talmid chacham*, why don't you hit me?" This seemed to stop him in his tracks, but then he turned around and grabbed a handful of my clothes from the bed, rushed down the stairs like a maniac, opened the front door, and threw my clothes into the middle of the street.

By this time I was sobbing uncontrollably while my sister stood by helplessly. I picked up my suitcase, retrieved my clothes from the street, and walked to Fela's flat, a few minutes' away, where Fela was now living with her mother and sister. They immediately took me into their cramped quarters, and I slept on the floor of their flat until the day I left for Israel.

CHAPTER SEVEN

ISRAEL

Traveling to Israel in December 1949 was not an easy undertaking for anyone, and especially not for a seventeen-year-old girl traveling alone. The whole journey was one of those bad dreams one would prefer to forget. First the rough Channel crossing from Dover to Calais; then the boat train to Paris's Gare du Nord; then a taxi to the Gare de Lyon to catch the train to Marseilles (with a rude taxi driver who pretended not to understand my carefully rehearsed French and took me for a tour of Paris to jack up his fare). On the overnight train to Marseilles I was lucky. I heard some Hebrew singing coming from down the corridor. When I went to investigate, I discovered a group of *chalutzim* (pioneers) fresh from their *hachsharah* training, on their way to a kibbutz in Israel. They asked me to join them, and some of the girls let me stay in their *pension* room in Marseilles when it became clear that our ship was not leaving immediately.

Finally we were able to board a ship, an old Italian tub that appeared barely seaworthy. A rough voyage followed, reminding me of the crossing I had taken years before from the Hook of Holland to Harwich. This, however, was a three-day voyage. My bunk was in the hold of the ship with about twenty other female passengers, mostly immigrants from Morocco and Algiers – women, children, and babies, many of them seasick for the whole voyage. The air in the hold became so foul and fetid that I found it impossible to stay down there. I spent many hours on deck in the fresh air. As a result of my absence from my bunk, some of my few possessions were stolen.

We arrived in Haifa harbor in the middle of the night, and the ship lay to until morning. The sight of dawn breaking over Mount Carmel and the rising sun glinting playfully on the house windows up and down the mountainside made the whole difficult voyage worthwhile. All the passengers lined the railings on the top deck and spontaneously began to sing the *Hatikvah*. It was a very emotional moment, and many tears were shed.

Small boats took us ashore, where I was met by a representative of the *Sochnut*, the Jewish Agency. They had found lodgings for me in Tel Binyamin near Ramat Gan, in a large house that had been converted into a Mizrachi hostel for girls. For two years I lived on the grounds of the house in a wooden hut with two other girls. One was Gail, a Londoner born and bred, and we became fast friends. The other girl was Ahuva, a concentration camp survivor from Hungary, who slipped in and out unobtrusively, like a shadow. The hut was mosquito-infested because of the small fishpond near the main house, and we were soon covered with bites all over our faces and bodies.

The Israeli foreign minister, Moshe Sharett, lived right next door, giving our location a certain cachet. We watched with great curiosity and interest as Mr. Sharett came and went in his important-looking car, on the hood of which the blue-and-white Israeli flag fluttered proudly. We cooked our meals in the hut on a Primus stove that ran on paraffin and were lucky that the whole place didn't go up in smoke and flames. I'm sure if Mr. Sharett's security people had known of the danger lurking just next door, they would have closed us down.

On the ship to Israel I had met and befriended a girl my age from Iraq. She was traveling with her husband who was not much older; they were making aliyah. The girl was pregnant with their first child, and she was sick for the entire voyage. When we made anchor in Haifa harbor, the husband told me that he and his wife were to spend their first weeks or months in Israel in a *ma'abarah*, an absorption camp for new immigrants. He and his wife were very nervous about the prospect, especially as she would most likely have to give birth in the camp. The young husband spoke to me in fairly good English; he had obviously received some form of education in Iraq. He begged me to try and visit them and bring his wife certain pharmaceutical items and foods that she craved. I remember one thing he asked for specifically was strawberry jam.

I took down their names and the address of the camp, which was just outside Tel Aviv near what was then Lydda airport. A few weeks later, after I myself had settled down and was working, I scraped together some money, shopped for a few items including strawberry jam (which was not easy to find in the new austerity-ridden state), and brought it to the *ma'abarah*. I found the young couple in a depressed state; they seemed to be angry with each other and barely on speaking terms. The young mother-to-be took me aside and expressed anger at her husband for having brought her to Israel; she longed for her parents back in Iraq and was homesick for the comfortable life she had led. She had obviously been a pretty girl, but now her face was puffy and sullen and she had a swollen belly that made it difficult for her to walk. She was not having an easy pregnancy; her nausea continued unabated even though she was now in her sixth or seventh month. She showed me the large tent in which they had to sleep with a score of others and in conditions that were at best squalid, and at worst barely fit for animals. It had rained recently and the water had seeped into the tent, turning the ground into a field of wet mud. That there was not an outbreak of typhoid, or worse, was a miracle. The husband, on the other hand, was angry and disappointed with his wife for her lack of support. He was a tall, good-looking young man with dark, piercing eyes and a shock of black hair. When I was about to leave, he accompanied me to the gate and told me in no uncertain terms how much he regretted his marriage. If it were not for the coming baby, he said, he would leave her. I did not feel qualified to comment. I felt sorry for them both but did not wish to be drawn any further into their affairs. They wrote to me, but I didn't reply, and I never saw them again.

*   *   *

I was lucky to find a job almost immediately with an insurance adjuster on Lilienthal Street in Tel Aviv. Mr. T. handled reparations from Germany, the *Wiedergutmachungs* claims, which brought so much German machinery and so many German buses and Mercedes-Benz cars into Israel. In the summer my office day began at seven-thirty and ended at two thirty. The heat was so intense that it was impossible to work beyond that; by noon my head was swimming and I had to rest it on my typewriter while sweat ran down my whole body and waves of heat danced before my eyes. There was no air conditioning anywhere, and if we wanted to cool off my friends and I went to the beach at Bat Yam or to a public swimming pool.

My boss, Mr. T., was a middle-aged Scotsman of average height with a pleasant, almost handsome face. During my job interview he charmed me with his Scottish lilt and Jewish warmth. I had not been working for him for more than a couple of weeks when I discovered why the job had been so readily available in a tight labor market. Mr. T. was a lecher, a sexual predator. I learned that since the opening of his insurance agency a few months earlier, he had had a steady parade of young secretaries, each of whom quit after a few weeks because of Mr. T.'s inappropriate advances. The fact that he had a perfectly nice wife and children, who sometimes dropped by the office, did not seem to deter him in the least. Because we were becoming so busy processing the increasingly heavy load of claims, Mr. T. also hired a male assistant, a concentration camp survivor who badly needed the job. This gentle and sensitive man became my protector and made sure I was rarely left alone in the office with Mr. T.

One day I wore to work a green jumper that I had knitted with yarn unraveled from the cardigan Mrs. Whyte-Smith had made for me years before and which, of course, I had outgrown. I was very proud of the result, especially of the zipper I had managed to install in the front opening of the jumper. My hands were full with a tray containing the hot coffee, milk, and sugar that Mr. T. had requested. As I neared his desk, he reached up from his chair and tried to pull down my zipper. I was so shocked that I dumped the whole tray and its contents into his lap. The hot coffee had a startling effect: Mr. T. never bothered me again. But from that day on I began looking for another job.

To make a little extra money, I worked two evenings a week for an author who was writing a fictionalized version of the story of King David and Batsheva. The man would pace the room, dictating to me at the typewriter as he paced. By the end of each session my fingers were sore from the effort of keeping up with him. Depressing the keys on his manual Underwood was much more punishing than working the electric typewriters that came much later, not to mention today's computer keyboards.

In the meantime, my new friend Gail met a South African accountant at the bank where she worked; he had come from Johannesburg to conduct an audit of the bank's books, and it was love at first sight. They married and she moved with him to Johannesburg.

Soon after my arrival in Israel, I located my cousin Mina, Tante Regina's oldest daughter. She and her husband, Aryeh, and their newborn baby girl were living in Tel Aviv in one room on Hayarkon Street, above a Tenuva restaurant. They welcomed me warmly and put up a collapsible bed in their one little room for me to spend the night. There was no embarrassment in our sleeping all together in the same room, with baby Ilana in her cot in the corner. They had no kitchen, no bathroom, no toilet. They had to go down corridors just to wash a plate. But somehow they managed. Shortly afterward, by virtue of Aryeh's veteran status (he had fought in the Haganah), they were assigned a flat in a new complex that had just gone up north of Tel Aviv, in Ramat Aviv.

Many food items were scarce and everyone carried ration cards. I was fortunate to have been issued a child's ration card (valid only until age eighteen), and so instead of the adult allowance of one egg per week, I received six. I was happy to give my eggs and some of my other ration coupons to my cousin, Mina, for the baby. The few occasions when we allowed ourselves an egg were so precious that we did not wait for each other to get served; we so much relished this rare delicacy prepared the way we liked it – scrambled, sunny-side up or soft-boiled – that good manners flew out the window.

Tel Aviv's central bus station, where I arrived each morning from Tel Binyamin, seemed to exist under a permanent cloud of dust kicked up by the Dan and Egged buses slipping in and out of their berths on mostly unpaved surfaces. This, combined with the cacophony of sounds coming from the numerous peddlers selling everything from jewelry to cotton thread; the newspaper hawkers screaming "*Yediot, Yediot Acharonot*"; the ubiquitous beggars with their hands outstretched; the medley of aromas spewing out of the falafel stands; the *mitz* kiosks on every corner selling freshly squeezed orange and grapefruit juice, which was for me a new and special treat – all this combined to create an ambience that I felt must exist only in this precious little corner of the world.

Sometimes on my walk to the office from the bus station, I'd notice that a section of Allenby Street was cordoned off. A platform was erected in the middle of the street, and on the platform stood an unadorned marriage canopy, a *chuppah* covered with a large tallit. A line of brides and grooms stood patiently waiting on the curb. They were waiting to get married. A rabbi stood beneath the *chuppah*, ready to perform the ceremonies. Sometimes the bride rushed off to the side right after the breaking of the glass, removed her white wedding gown behind a screen, and quickly passed it on to the next bride. However, most of the brides did not wear white wedding gowns but dressed in plain suits or frocks, and the only celebratory symbols to be seen were nosegays in the groom's lapel or a small corsage held by the bride. These couples were all survivors of the concentration camps, recently arrived from Europe, where they had spent several years in displaced persons camps. Most of them took their wedding vows without any family present; all their relatives had perished in the Holocaust. Their witnesses were strangers plucked off the street. These young survivors were picking up the ruins of their lives and going on. I cannot imagine a stranger or more surreal assembly line, both happy and sad at the same time. All the onlookers, I among them, shouted *"Mazal tov, mazal tov"* after each bridegroom smashed the glass with his foot.

*   *   *

I connected with some of the old Sheffordians, and sometimes a few of us would spend Shabbat at the religious Mizrachi kibbutzim where some of our old schoolmates had settled: Ein Hanatziv, Tirat Zvi, Lavi. To reach the kibbutzim we always hitchhiked; we were not afraid and it was never a problem to find an obliging lorry driver or army jeep to take us to our destination. I met up again with Dora, who was still singing away; she later joined the army and married a fellow soldier. I met Gypsy, who had a secretarial job in Haifa. I found Hedy again, who had forgotten all about redheaded Joe and later married a handsome Moroccan policeman; and Renate, who had served as a nurse in the War of Independence and afterward went back to England to marry her old sweetheart, Chaim. Rita, also a nurse, married

Henry, another German refugee who had lived in London and been a regular visitor to our hostel.

Shabbat meals at the kibbutzim with all the singing and *horah* dancing reminded me nostalgically of our communal life in Shefford, but much as I loved visiting the kibbutzim, I knew that kibbutz life was not for me. When I learned that the legs of our sleeping cots had to rest in bowls of water to discourage the scorpions that abounded in the area, I knew with certainty that I was a confirmed city girl.

Those hitched rides to the kibbutzim gave me a chance to see a little of the country, and as I sat in the back of an open lorry on the way to the She'an Valley, I could not help but be overtaken by the history of the land. To my right, Mount Gilboa, where King David had fought and hidden from King Saul in a cave; to the north, Mount Carmel, where the prophet Elijah had offered sacrifices and preached to the people about false gods. Every inch of ground was soaked with the history of our people. Was this the path traveled by Abraham? The road taken by Samson?

On a trip to Jerusalem that lasted only a few hours because I knew no one there and had nowhere to stay (I couldn't afford a hotel), I was saddened not to be able to go to the Western Wall, which was in Jordanian hands. I climbed up to the roof of the YMCA building opposite the King David Hotel just to get a glimpse of the Wall and the Old City. So near and yet so far. Some of the buildings were visibly pockmarked with bullet holes, evidence of the fighting that had taken place not long before, but everywhere I went they were building and building, bulldozing, repairing, and scaffolding.

When walking the streets of Tel Aviv, and during my visit to Jerusalem and my occasional visits to Haifa, I found myself scanning the faces of passersby, especially those of bearded men. I had not yet let go of the absurd, childish fantasy I'd developed in the hostel after the war: the one that had my parents reaching Palestine but suffering from amnesia. It was totally irrational. For not only did I not remember what my parents had looked like at our parting in 1938, I certainly had no idea what they would have looked like after so many years. Yet I persisted in this bizarre habit until the day I left the country.

*   *   *

In May of 1950 my friends and I rejoiced with the whole country as we celebrated the second *Yom Atzma'ut*, Israel's Independence Day. We went down to the Tel Aviv beach at night and joined in the *horah* dancing and singing. The beach was lit up from one end to the other with a string of bonfires, and every now and then low-flying airplanes with the proud Star of David symbol on their wings flew overhead and dipped their wings in salute. Some of the people on the beach were old-timers who had arrived in Palestine many years earlier and were the *chalutzim* who had cleared the swamps and irrigated the desert – the builders of the nascent state. Many were survivors of the concentration camps; others were survivors of the recent war that had led to this celebration. Strangers embraced and hugged and kissed each other. We were all one happy family. One happy Jewish family.

After a few months I found a job much more to my liking. This time I was *really* lucky. I was hired by the British Council, the educational arm of the British Consulate. One of the functions of the British Council was to hold examinations for British nationals living overseas, a task I enjoyed immensely. I was particularly happy with the enormous library housed in the Council's offices on Allenby Street near Mugrabi Square, and I was forever ransacking the shelves for new reading material. One of the other girls in the office, Fira, with whom I became friendly, was born in China, the daughter of White Russians who had fled to China to escape the Russian revolution. Having led a privileged life in Tientsin for many years, Fira's family had to flee once again, this time from the encroaching Communist regime of Mao Tse Tung. Fira and the other girls in the office were Jewish, but the two directors of the

Council were British gentiles. I was therefore not too surprised when we were all invited to an office Christmas party at the British Consulate, though it did seem a bit incongruous to be attending a Christmas party in the Jewish state.

A modest Christmas tree on display in a corner of the consul's office was adorned with the usual ornaments and strung with colored lights that twinkled merrily away and, of course, the requisite glittering angel to top it off. I had never tasted hard spirits but was determined to show how grown-up I was. And so, when the consul asked me what I would like to drink, the only name that sprung to mind was cognac, and that is what I requested. He raised his eyebrows in surprise and said, "Are you quite sure, my dear?" I put on my best sophisticated air and answered, "Of course," as if I had been used to drinking cognac all my life. Fortunately I didn't like the stuff; to me it had a medicinal aftertaste, and so I barely sipped at my glass before setting it down. I noticed the consul watching me with a smile, but he was very tactful and said not a word. Later I found out that cognac has a high alcohol content and is very potent. Who knows what would have happened if I had drunk a couple of shots of it!

Fira later became engaged to one of the gentile directors of the British Council; subsequently she broke that engagement and took up with another gentile man who worked for one of the British airlines. She married him and the last I heard they were living in Lima, Peru.

EPILOGUE

I returned to London in 1952 in a propeller plane, a journey that was a lot different from the one I had taken to Israel by ship over two years before. My decision to return was made after I learned that I was eligible for military service and would soon be drafted. At that time I was not sure that I was strong enough in my religious convictions to withstand the influences and temptations that were rumored to be rampant in the Israeli army. I was not happy to leave Israel, despite the austerity that existed and the hardships I saw my cousins endure just to make ends meet and put food on the table. To be surrounded by my own people, to be among Jews all day, every day, was a feeling of belonging such as I had never experienced before, even in Shefford, and I vowed to myself that one day I would come back and settle permanently in the Jewish state. (Ah, the best-laid plans of mice and men…!)

I came back to London with well-honed secretarial skills and an impeccable reference from the British Council. I found a job in the City with an international trading company owned by Orthodox Jews. (The president of the head office in New York was none other than the late philanthropist, Ludwig Jesselson.)

I took a room with a family in Golders Green. If I could have found a Jewish neighborhood even farther away from my poor sister Miriam's tyrannical husband, I would have moved there. I had lodged at my sister's house for a few nights directly after my return from Israel and couldn't wait to leave. During my absence from England, my sister had finally given birth, after seven barren years, to a lovely little boy. This naturally raised her status by several notches in the eyes of her husband. But the raise was only temporary and didn't last very long. He was as domineering as ever. As for me, though he claimed to be happy that I had left the *treife medinah*, as he called it, "the nonkosher Jewish state," he taunted me endlessly about my recent sojourn in Israel. I gave a huge sigh of relief when I was finally able to move to my own place on the other side of London.

Soon after my return to London, King George the Sixth died and his elder daughter, Princess Elizabeth, was crowned Queen of England. The coronation ceremony was held in Westminster Abbey, and like her wedding ceremony, the film was simultaneously shown in all the London cinemas. A national holiday was declared. For two or three days after the coronation the new queen and her consort, Prince Philip, toured different areas of London in an open car and waved to the crowds lining the streets. My office also sent us out to show our respect for the new queen, and even though I was impressed by Elizabeth's beautiful "peaches and cream" complexion and her charming smile, I couldn't help remembering Annie's words: *Poor little buggers. I wouldn't want to be in their shoes for all the tea in China.*

In 1953 Cousin Mina wrote that she and Aryeh and Ilana were leaving Israel and moving to New York. Not only had the economic situation worsened for them, but Tante Regina was clamoring to be reunited with her oldest daughter, whom she had not seen since their parting in 1938, and to meet her son-in-law and new granddaughter. I was saddened to hear that after so many years of "roughing it," and after Aryeh had risked his life in the War of Independence, they felt they could no longer make a go of it in Israel. For Aryeh the wrench of leaving Israel was much greater than for Mina, because he was leaving his father and siblings behind. But it was one thing to rough it for themselves, quite another with a child involved.

In 1954 one of the directors of the New York office visited the London office and I was assigned to help him out with secretarial duties during his stay. Before he returned to New York, he asked me if I would be interested in coming to work for him in New York. I didn't have to think twice. I immediately wrote to Tante Regina and asked if she would be willing to sponsor me, and she obligingly sent me an affidavit.

* * *

I sailed for New York on the Cunard Line's *Queen Mary*, the ship that today is a tourist attraction in Long Beach Harbor in California. This voyage was a far cry from the one I had taken from Marseilles to Haifa over five years earlier. I shared a comfortable cabin with one other woman, and even though the ocean was stormy because it was the equinox season, the big ship's stabilizers kept the rolling to a minimum. The ship had a kosher kitchen and a separate area in the dining room for passengers who wished to have kosher meals. Mr. Oscar Philipp, the head of the London office, had alerted the ship's purser that I was on board. Because of his many transatlantic crossings, Mr. Philipp was well acquainted with the captain and purser. On our second day out, the purser knocked on the door of my cabin and handed me an invitation to dine at the captain's table that night. I was very excited to be honored in this way. As luck would have it, just that evening I became seasick for the first time and could not keep the engagement.

We sailed into New York's harbor in calm waters on a radiant morning in March. The air was crisp and clear showing off the Manhattan skyline in all its skyscraper awesomeness. The tugboats guided and towed the Queen Mary into her berth, with a lot of tooting and blowing of horns. In the distance, to our left, Lady Liberty welcomed us with her torch held aloft. I was familiar with "The New Colossus," the Emma Lazarus poem etched into the statue's pedestal, and could not help being relieved that I was arriving in New York in style, and not as one of those hordes of "huddled masses, yearning to breathe free" who had come through Ellis Island in the first quarter of the century as hopeful refugees. Once again, I found myself comparing. I thought back to that day over five years earlier, when I had arrived in Haifa harbor in an old, barely seaworthy tub. And I realized that undeniably exciting though it was to be arriving in America, I was not moved by the same emotions that had overwhelmed me upon arriving in the Holy Land.

Tante Regina and Mina and my two other Greisman cousins, Tonka and Dorrit, were at the New York dock to greet me. In England poor Princess Margaret was experiencing a showdown with her sister Queen Elizabeth, who forbade Margaret to marry the divorced Peter Townsend. No sooner had I set foot off the ship than Tante Regina, who by virtue of her short stay in England had become an inveterate Anglophile and a fanatic royalist, greeted me rather impatiently and then asked, "*Nu*, so? What's with Margaret?" – as if I was in the princess's confidence and had firsthand knowledge of her love life!

I soon found out that Tante Regina was now also a proud *Yenkeedoodle*, which is how she referred to herself. She had been taking English classes at night and had recently learned about Columbus Day. She ended up educating the teacher. She raised her hand in class, and when the teacher called on her said, "Teacher, Christopher Columbus, he save ze Jews." The teacher, nonplussed, naturally inquired how Christopher Columbus had managed to accomplish this amazing feat. Tante Regina answered with assurance, "Teacher, if not Columbus he discover America, all ze Jews be killed." Who could argue with that logic?

Tante Regina was also a regular visitor to the Yiddish theaters on the East Side. Her favorite actress was Molly Picon. When she learned that Miss Picon was scheduled to visit Poland, my aunt somehow managed to finagle her way into the star's dressing room. Once there, she informed the startled actress that her husband (Onkel Pinchas) had gone back to Poland in 1938 and had not been heard from again. She requested that Miss Picon try to find out what had happened to him. The actress was extremely kind and took down all the pertinent information in my aunt's possession. I believe Miss Picon actually did make some inquiries in Poland regarding Onkel Pinchas' fate, but her efforts met a dead end.

Soon after my arrival in New York, I also contacted and visited Tante Rosa and Onkel Benno. It was not a successful visit. Tante Rosa was still so riddled with jealousy toward her sister that she couldn't come to terms with the fact that Tante Regina had sponsored my entry into the United States. She grumbled that I should have asked her instead. I did find it amusing though, when Tante Rosa, with her thick German accent, corrected my English pronunciation of certain words like *aluminum* and *specialty* and *controversy*. She particularly cautioned me against using the word *fortnight*. "No vun in America uses zat vort. You must say two veeks!" The last nail in the coffin of our relationship was hammered in when Tante Rosa served me a dinner that she assured me had been provided by the strictly kosher delicatessen on the corner. After I finished eating she said, "Vell, let me tell you, zose hot dogs vere *not* kosher. Could you taste ze difference?" To this day I am not sure if she was really capable of such a wicked deception; I prefer to think that the food she served was kosher and that she was merely guilty of a twisted and cruel sense of humor. Except for inviting Tante Rosa and Onkel Benno to my wedding, I had very little further contact with them.

Poor Tante Rosa. She and I would have made a perfect *shidduch*, a perfect match. She had no children; I had no parents. We could and should have been a comfort to each other. I am still not sure whether her attitude toward me was one of disdain for my religious practices or whether her jealousy toward her sister was so overpowering that it created an insurmountable obstacle to any form of affection or intimacy between us.

As for Tante Hanni, the youngest of my three aunts, when she became a widow, she and her son Peter left Buenos Aires and made aliyah; they settled in Beersheba. She stuck to her left-wing, agnostic principles to the very end, and left strict instructions in her will that her body be cremated. Which it was – in Israel, of all places.

In New York I naturally also contacted our cousin Fritz Horowitz, my only Horowitz relative to survive the war. We had a lot of trouble tracking him down after the war ended because he had changed his name. After Pearl Harbor, Fritz joined the United States Army and, because of his fluency in German, was assigned to a special intelligence unit where he interrogated German prisoners of war. Not wishing to draw attention to his German first name and Jewish surname, he became Fred Howard. Fred had married Ilse, a German refugee who grew up in Colombia. Just before I arrived in New York, Ilse gave birth to a baby girl.

I located my old Cardiff and Shefford friend, Edith, with whom I had maintained sporadic correspondence ever since she left for America after the war. She was not long married and, like Ilse, had recently given birth to a baby girl. Edith's husband, Henry, was a German refugee, a survivor of the camps, with a telltale tattoo on his arm. Their apartment became a sanctuary for me, a refuge to escape to for Shabbat and Jewish holidays whenever I was so inclined, which was very often. These two war orphans had miraculously found each other and together built a beautiful life and family on the ashes of the Holocaust.

At around this time, my brother Ephraim married a lovely girl from a Chassidic family in Gateshead, England. Though they met through a *shidduch*, an arranged match, their marriage was a true love affair. They settled in London and their family thrived. Besides having inherited our Opa Shmuel's looks, modesty, and many of his other fine qualities, Ephraim also inherited Opa Shmuel's business acumen. He became a successful businessman, known for his piety and quiet philanthropy.

I found my job sometimes challenging but more often tedious. It was, however, a great convenience to be working for a firm owned and run by Orthodox Jews. As a result I had no problem taking time off for the Jewish holidays and leaving the office early on Fridays in the winter. When Mr. Philipp came to New York on business, he always asked for my secretarial services during his stay, and those visits were a welcome interlude. Mr. Philipp was a pint-sized little man with an almost bald head and courtly manners. He was always impeccably outfitted in a three-piece, dark gray or black pin-stripe suit. His fingernails were manicured and he reeked of cologne, which he ordered by the gallon from his wife's family in Paris, the Weils of the perfume industry.

When I had worked for the firm in London, Mr. Philipp had shown a special interest in me. He often invited me to Shabbat dinners at his sprawling brick house on Hampstead Heath, which was within easy walking distance of my rented room in Golders Green. Once, on a Sunday morning, he and his wife Clarissa picked me up in their chauffeured Bentley and drove me out to a *hachsharah* farm outside London that the Philipps supported financially. Mrs. Philipp was a warm, grandmotherly woman without any airs or snobbery to her. At the farm, they were both proud to show me around and point out the work that was being done by the *chalutzim*, who would eventually make aliyah. It was harvest time, and I was fascinated by the tractors and the other machinery used to bring in and bundle sheaves of wheat. When we were strolling through the cow stalls, Mrs. Philipp pointed with special pride to a cow that had been named for her. Above the animal's stall, printed in large letters, was the name: Clarissa. The chauffeur unpacked a very ample lunch from a picnic hamper, and we ate at a table in the shade of an oak tree.

However at the Friday night dinners in the Philipps' home, a butler and maid served a meal that always left me hungry. One potato, one small slice of meat, and one spoonful of peas were just not enough to assuage my healthy appetite. Mr. Philipp was very proud of the new instant coffee that had just come on the market. He said it was very difficult to obtain and he had had it shipped over from Switzerland. The butler came into the dining room bearing a silver tray on which sat, in all its solitary glory, a small tin that proudly trumpeted the name of this hard-to-get beverage: Nestcafé.

The Philipps had two sons, both medical doctors. I did not have the opportunity to meet the older son Elliot until many years later, at a function in Los Angeles. Elliot was one of the pioneers in the field of *in vitro* fertilization and one of the team responsible for the first baby born by this method in England. The younger son, Anthony, a man of about forty, lived with his parents and was always present at the Friday night dinners, where he sat with his head down, rarely opening his mouth to speak. Anthony had once been a successful doctor but had not practiced medicine since the end of the war. It was rumored that he had suffered some kind of mental breakdown in the Burma theater. Supposedly his unit had been cut off by the enemy from the main Allied forces and they had run out of drugs, such as quinine for the malaria that was rampant in the region. Not being able to help the injured and wounded had affected Anthony so deeply that he could no longer function as a physician. Apparently he never went out in daylight; he just roamed the London streets at night. At times I suspected that Mr. Philipp was hoping for something romantic to develop between Anthony and me. Perhaps he thought that as an orphan I might be grateful to marry a man twice my age, damaged or not, and one who had the Philipp wealth behind him. However I was not interested in Anthony and he never showed the slightest interest in me either.

One day, on one of his visits to New York, Mr. Philipp asked me to accompany him to Saks Fifth Avenue; he wished to buy one of the new "in" fake furs for his wife, Clarissa (who probably had a wardrobe full of real furs), and wanted me to help him pick one out. In the store I tried on and modeled several "fur" coats and jackets for Mr. Philipp, and I thought it very rude of the two salesgirls helping us to be snickering behind their hands. At the time I thought they were laughing at Mr. Philipp's appearance. It was only later that it occurred to me that they must have thought Mr. Philipp was my sugar-daddy and that the coat he ended up buying was for me!

Mr. Jesselson, too, seemed to take a special interest in me. On a couple of occasions he invited me to share a Shabbat meal with his family in their spacious apartment on Riverside Drive. He once talked about fixing me up on a blind date, but nothing ever came of it. In the office I sat just two low partitions away from the now-infamous and very wealthy international fugitive, Marc Rich. In those days Marc was a slender, good-looking, dark-haired young man who drove a flashy red convertible sports car. It was obvious even then that Marc was considered to be the firm's fair-haired boy, destined for great things in the world of commodities trading. Naturally, he had no time to talk to lowly secretaries.

By this time I had met many eligible young men and dated more than a few, both in London and in New York. At first I thought I would have more in common with a European rather than with an American-born man because of the similarity of backgrounds. After a while, however, I began to feel a sense of oppression whenever I went out with a boy whose history was similar to mine. The mournful stories of death and loss began to weigh on me. I realized that I did not want to commiserate or wallow in these boys' tales of suffering. A parentless past was just not enough of a common bond to create a meaningful relationship. On the other hand, the Orthodox American boys I went out with, especially the Yeshiva University types, were attractive to me because of their "normalcy," their healthy, uncomplicated childhoods, their fine education, their positive attitude to life. Their mothers, however, were a different story. As soon as one of the mothers of these American young men suspected her boy might be getting serious about a "ref," a refugee, the relationship was immediately nipped in the bud. (The first time I heard the word *ref*, I thought it was shorthand for the referee of the Brooklyn Dodgers!)

One of the young men I went out with for a couple of months was a newly ordained Y.U. rabbi. He had a great sense of humor and we enjoyed each other's company. It took me a while to catch on to the fact that he was "cheap." Whenever we rode in his car and came to a toll booth, he suddenly had no change; when we rode on the subway, he searched his pockets fruitlessly for change for tokens. So, naturally, I paid. I thought perhaps he just had no money and was embarrassed to admit it. Then came the night he took me to dinner. Not wanting him to spend a lot of money on me, I asked him to recommend something from the menu. He said the omelets were very good. I ordered a mushroom omelet. He ordered a steak! In his case, I didn't wait to hear his mother's opinion about "refs." Needless to say, that was our last date.

In 1959 I met Lenny, the man I would marry. He was American-born, with what I call a "normal" background, from a "normal" home, with two loving European parents. His parents kept a traditional Jewish home, kosher but not Sabbath-observant. We met on a blind date set up by Mina and Aryeh. It turned out that Aryeh's father and Lenny's mother were first cousins who had not seen each other since they were children in Lodz, Poland. Before agreeing to marry Lenny, I told him I wanted us not only to have a kosher home, but to observe Shabbat, and if we were blessed with children, to educate them in Jewish day schools. He agreed, and in 1960 we married and started our family. In 1972 Lenny's work as an attorney for the American Broadcasting Companies brought us and our three children to Los Angeles.

*   *   *

In 1973, twenty-eight years after the end of the war, we received the news. A mass grave had been uncovered in Brko, Yugoslavia. Thanks to the German obsession with record-keeping, a list existed. On it were the names of two hundred Viennese Jews, among them my parents and my father's mother, Oma Blima. The grave was disinterred and the remains transferred to the Jewish cemetery in Vienna and given a proper Jewish burial according to *Halachah* by the Vienna *Chevra Kadisha* (Jewish burial society).

Subsequently, Lenny and I traveled to Vienna to visit the cemetery. This was my first visit to the city of my birth since I had left it on the *Kindertransport* in December 1938. I refused to stay in an Austrian hotel; I was determined to leave as little money as possible in Austria. We were lucky to find a kosher *pension* that served our needs and was, coincidentally, not far from my family's old flat on the Heinzelmangasse. On the afternoon of our arrival in Vienna, we walked over to my old apartment building. It looked much different in real life than in my memory, not nearly as tall and much more elegant. The neighborhood must have undergone a face-lift since we lived there; it looked almost upscale. We rang the bell for the concierge. I recalled no such thing as a bell or a concierge from my childhood. After we were buzzed in, I told the young woman at the desk that my family had lived in the building before the war and I was curious to see our old flat. In a distinctly hostile and brusque manner, she told me that the flat was occupied and she could not let us in. I asked her if we could at least go upstairs and look at the door of our flat. She was clearly puzzled by my request but, with obvious reluctance, allowed us to walk up the stairs to the first floor. I don't know what I expected to find – certainly not the shadowy outline of a mezuzah that was still plainly visible on the doorpost of my childhood home. I stared and stared at that mezuzah imprint, as if transfixed. How many times, I wondered, had my father's fingers lingered on that spot? We walked down the block and I looked for signs of our grocery shop and my father's *shtiebel*. It was as if they had never existed; in their place stood a mattress shop and another business of some kind.

In the kosher restaurant that evening we met an old Jewish man with sad eyes. We spoke in Yiddish, and when he heard my maiden name his sad eyes lit up with recognition. "I knew your grandfather," he said. "We used to *daven* in the same *shtiebel* on the Taborstrasse not far from here," and he waved his hand in the direction of the Taborstrasse. He himself was a survivor of the camps; he rolled up his sleeve to show us the number tattooed on his arm. He had watched his wife and children taken to their deaths, and had come back to Vienna after the war because, he explained, that was the only place familiar to him – although, he said, shrugging his shoulders, one place would have been as good as another after what he had experienced. And yes, he added, he had heard of the mass grave of Viennese Jews uncovered in Yugoslavia. "The bodies were found with their hands and feet bound," he said.

The Vienna public transportation network is run on the honor system. Tickets or tokens are sold in various shops, such as newsstands, and there are spot checks on trams and buses and in the metro, with the threat of a hefty fine should anyone be discovered traveling without a ticket. I took wicked pleasure in riding on the trams and the metro without paying. If we were stopped, I planned to profess ignorance of the system and the language. I was childishly disappointed that we were not subjected to a spot check.

We rode by tram to the Zentralfriedhof, the huge cemetery that covers over two square miles and consists of several sections for different religious denominations, including two Jewish sections. I had been directed to Section Four, and the tram took us almost to the gate. Because my husband is a *kohen*, he was unable to enter and had to wait for me outside. It was a miserable, cold and grey February afternoon, and as I wandered by myself among the tombstones with their Jewish names and markings, their histories and soulful epitaphs, a steady, persistent drizzle came down, the kind that seeps right into the bones. It took me some time to locate the grave, and by the time I found it, the rain was coming down in earnest. I had no umbrella and was glad of it. To have been protected from the elements at that moment would, I think, have felt obscene. The stone is a plain flat slab set flush with the earth, which is why it was difficult to find. It merely states that the grave contains the remains of the Viennese Jews killed by the Nazis in Brko, Yugoslavia, on such and such date.

In the pouring rain, I recited the Kaddish.

THE DEED

Your faces in shadow, always in shadow,
Turned away from me,
As if unable to confront the deed,
That inhuman deed.

What anguish was poured into our valises,
What pain in every pleat and fold,
Each sock, each precious sock
Awash with tears.
Tell me, Mama, tell me Papa,
Whence came the courage, from where the will
To send your babies on that train?
Babes who yesterday suckled at their mother's breast,
Whose hurts you soothed,
Whose laughter you absorbed
In joy and sorrow.
Babes you birthed a second time
When you hurled them
Into the void,
By that inhuman deed.

Grieve no more Papa, weep no more Mama.
It is we who must grieve. Do grieve.
We who, with shuttered eyes, dare not imagine
The unimaginable.
They found you later, much later,
Bound like heifers before slaughter,
Hands first then shackled feet.
Immobilized.
Would you have struggled?
Fought against your fate?
No. Impossible.
For you did not even rail against the One,

But shouted His name until the very end
With unfettered faith. Even joy.
Of that I am certain.
Impossible to imagine less.
Impossible to imagine more.
The screen goes black.

Is there a day we have not yearned for you
Who sowed four seeds but never saw them grow,
Nor barely tilled the soil that rooted them?
Rich soil it was, and fertile, too,
For though you watered little, you watered well.
Hardy, those four seeds you planted long ago.
Seeds that sprouted sprigs and twigs, leaves and branches,
Too numerous to count, too treasured not to.
Each honored with the burden of memory
In its name.
Each faithful to the map laid out by you
And ancestors.
Ancestors of Sinaic ancestors.

Dearest Papa, brave and precious Mama.
Come out from the shadows,
Turn your faces to me
So I can show you a hundred reasons
Not to grieve
But to rejoice
In that inhuman deed.

—Frieda Stolzberg Korobkin

AFTERWORD

(Adapted from the writer's article in
Amit Magazine, *Spring 2000)*

In the spring of 1999 I learn that a reunion is to take place in London that summer to celebrate the sixtieth anniversary of the *Kindertransports*. I decide this is something I should attend, perhaps with my whole family.

My husband tells me he can't get away for business reasons but feels our children might benefit from the experience. I invite all three of them to come with me. My daughter, the oldest, declines the invitation. Jennifer feels she will not be able to handle the emotions that the reunion will unleash. She has always had trouble dealing with my past, even though I rarely talked about the war when the children were growing up, and then only in answer to their specific questions. She, especially, has a problem with trains; in fact, she once told me that the idea of traveling anywhere by train agitates her. She believes this to be a reaction to stories of my early train journeys. Jennifer has become an energetic community activist and I am proud of the many people she has influenced and brought back to *Yiddishkeit* as a direct result of her work as a real estate broker.

My sons Daniel and Samuel, with the approval of their respective wives, decide to accompany me. Daniel actually bears my father's name, Nissan, while Samuel is, of course, Shmuel, named for my paternal grandfather. At this time, Daniel is a pulpit rabbi in Allentown, Pennsylvania; Sam is a clinical psychologist in Baltimore, Maryland. Each, in his own way, a healer of souls.

I take the "red-eye" from Los Angeles, and the three of us meet at Kennedy airport in New York. As our Boeing 767 heads out over the "pond," I cannot help harking back to that long-ago journey and contrasting the comfort of this airplane with the conditions under which I traveled from Vienna to London so many years before.

But that was sixty years ago, and since then much water, not to mention blood, has flowed down the Danube, the Rhine, and the Vltava rivers. And now the aging, and in some cases ailing, survivors of those transports – some, like me, accompanied by children, others by grandchildren – were coming together in London for a reunion. We were arriving from Australia and Argentina, from the United States and Israel, to celebrate our survival and to affirm to the whole world the triumph over evil that our survival and our numerous progeny signify.

My sons and I arrive at our hotel late at night, weary from the long flight but filled with excited anticipation. The hotel is conveniently situated in Russell Square, surrounded by the University of London, where all our meetings are to be held. In the morning we make our way across the street to Logan Hall for registration. The place is packed with people wearing identification tags that bear their name and city of birth. Eventually the thirteen hundred attendees get sorted out and settle down in the auditorium for the keynote addresses.

The invocation is given by Chief Rabbi Jonathan Sacks. He quotes Robert Frost in describing home as "a place where they have to let you in." But, he continues, there was no home for the Jews in 1938 and 1939. Then Britain made the decision to admit ten thousand children from Germany, Austria, and Czechoslovakia and gave them the gift of life. England he says, quoting the prophet Hosea, was a *petach tikvah*, a valley of hope. He speaks of train journeys, some to death and some, like the *Kindertransports*, to life. He recalls the decency of the British people and individual acts of courage. Each of you, he says, addressing us, has given something unique to the world and given back the kindness once given you. He concludes: "The nation that begins by destroying others ends by destroying itself."

We are bidden to stand for the memorial service. Thirteen hundred voices rise as one to recite *Kel Maleh Rachamim* followed by Kaddish for parents and other loved ones murdered by the Nazis. In unison we read the following:

As we recite Kaddish, we also have in mind those of our fellow Kinder *who have gone to their eternal home. We give thanks for the gift of continued life which they, too, received when they were enabled to escape from the lands of the inferno; and whether or not we knew them, we pray that what was good in their lives may endure as a source of blessing.* Zichronam livracha *(may their memories be blessed).*

There is not a dry eye in the auditorium.

Lord Greville Janner, a Jew, injects some light relief by explaining to the non-Jewish Lord Richard Attenborough what a *simchah* is. A *simchah*, he says, is a reunion of thirteen hundred Jews all agreeing with each other! He describes his experiences as an eighteen-year-old prosecutorial assistant bringing war criminals to justice in Germany after the war, and he expresses the hope that we can create a world for others in which they will not go through what we did.

Lord Janner is followed by Lord Williams, minister of state for the Home Office of Great Britain, who proclaims his view that the "beast" of anti-Semitism and fascism never dies, just seems to sleep. That is why, he says, what happens in Kosovo is our business. It is dismal to think, he says, that sixty years later, other children far away don't have a home, a school, parents, or a settled, decent life.

One of the highlights of the morning is Lord Richard Attenborough, the illustrious one-time actor and director/producer of the motion picture *Gandhi*. He speaks, he says, on behalf of all the British families who went to the aid of the Jewish children in 1938–39, as his own family did. He speaks admiringly of his mother, who began her rescue efforts by saving Basque children during the Spanish Civil War. His father, a professor at Leicester University, began his rescue operations by bringing over academic colleagues at the outbreak of war and finding positions for them in British universities.

Soon, Lord Attenborough says, his parents were bringing children out of Germany, and there ensued a constant stream of young refugees coming and going through his parental home. One day, his father summoned Richard and his brother to his study to talk to them about two girls who were under their temporary care. "Boys," he said, "your mother and I have a very difficult decision to make. Helga and Irene have no relatives and nowhere to go. We wish to adopt them until after the war or until someone turns up to claim them. However we will not do so without your consent because this decision will affect your lives. There will be hardships and jealousies. For you see, boys, there may be times when we will have to show Helga and Irene more love than we show you because they have no one and they will need it more."

With tears streaming down his cheeks, Lord Attenborough relates how Helga and Irene became part of the Attenborough family; how Irene died some years after the war, but that Helga married, had children, and that he has stayed in close touch with her.

Lord Attenborough receives a standing ovation.

Emotionally drained and jet-lagged, we are happy to break

for lunch. The tables in the hotel dining room each bear the name of a town. My sons and I sit with friends at a Frankfurt table. I meet people I have not seen in forty years or more and experience one joyous reunion after another. I meet Rivka, one of the "hidden children," a girl from one of Rabbi Schonfeld's postwar transports. She shows me an old autograph book in which I had written: *If ever you need a friend, I will be here for you.* I am touched that she still has this memento. Today, Rivka and her family are members of the Lubavitch community in Crown Heights, Brooklyn.

I meet Richard Kaufman, an engineer, who had been a young man when we were in the hostel right after the war and who, to make a little money while he was going to engineering school, had taken on the unenviable task of supervising us each night while we did our homework in the common room. Part of Richard's job was also to make sure none of us left the hostel grounds at night without permission. I now apologize to Richard for the trouble I must have caused him in those distant days. For, certainly, I and some of my friends did not always obey the rules and often sneaked out to a movie at night, leaving poor Richard to answer to Miss D. when our absence was discovered.

In the afternoon, we hear a very moving talk by Stephen Smith, director of the Beth Shalom Holocaust Centre, and possibly the only non-Jewish director of such a facility in the world. Try to imagine, he says, the unimaginable. How a child feels, torn from the bosom of a warm and loving family, only to find himself, literally overnight, in a strange home, surrounded by a strange culture, having to learn a strange language. Imagine, if you can, how that child feels, lying in bed at night in his strange surroundings, no longer feeling that familiar, loving hand tucking him in, and in the darkness making his bargain with God: *If I am extra good, will You bring my parents back to me?* He speaks of the superhuman courage and sacrifice of the parents who sent their children into the unknown. Those who gave you life, he says, gave you a second chance at life.

Of the thirteen hundred attendees, it is difficult to know how many are Orthodox. Even though all the meals are strictly kosher, there are very few yarmulkes to be seen. After dinner, I am proud to notice my son, the rabbi, organizing an evening service. He also arranges for a room to be allocated for morning prayers.

About twenty of us gather in a small meeting room at the hotel. We are all "*Kinder*" of the late Rabbi Solomon Schonfeld, the man responsible for rescuing one thousand Orthodox children. We are here to trade stories and reminiscences about him. Rabbi Schonfeld's son, Jonathan, joins us and adds his own recollections to ours. Someone mentions how Rabbi Schonfeld was only twenty-six years old and unmarried in 1938 when he decided to go on a one-man rescue mission to save Jewish children in Europe. I relate the story my sons have heard before: how Rabbi Schonfeld always teased me about my Yiddish retort to him when I first met him as a child: "Throw your feet over your shoulders and run away."

On the second day, Lady Jakobovits, the wife of the former chief rabbi of Great Britain, Rabbi Immanuel Jakobovits, and an accomplished and mesmerizing speaker in her own right, moves her audience to tears as she speaks of the faith that saw her family through their wartime ordeal hiding in Occupied France; of how their friends were aghast at her parents for continuing to have children during the war, and how her one-year-old brother saved their lives at the Swiss border by crying at the right time and drawing the attention of a compassionate Swiss guard, who led them all to safety.

Later my sons participate in an informal discussion group for second- and third-generation *Kinder*, who share a universal sense of loss at having grown up without grandparents.

We take fond leave of our friends, old and new, and go on a bus excursion to Bath and Stonehenge. All three of us are suffering from emotional overload, and this outing provides a sorely needed respite. As the bus rumbles through the lush, green English countryside, I am suddenly jolted by the realization of how much I love this "fair and pleasant land," this land that made my life possible. Unbidden, I recall how whenever I undergo an unpleasant dental procedure, I recite to myself with wry masochism the famous poem by Rupert Brooke that begins: "If I should die, think only this of me/That there's some corner of a foreign field/That is for ever England…"

That thought is followed by the memory of a much, much lesser poem, a sonnet I wrote for a class assignment many moons ago. It is titled "A Penitent's Plea" and still sums up my feelings perfectly.

> A splendid star were you 'mid vilest dark
> When all around were sinking in the mire
> Of infamy. A hand outstretched, a spark
> Of sanity that plucked me from the pyre.
> Your love held constant through that tortured night,
> But, when dawn upon the ruins rose
> And Liberty beckoned from briny height,
> I turned away without remorse from Eros
> And his friends: the Duke, the Admiral, St. Paul.
> A fickle lover, I, who spurned you on a whim,
> To blindly serve that siren's call,
> And nail down fealty in casket dim.
> Yet, now you greet me sans reproach or chill.
> Oh England! Dare I love you still?

PHOTO ALBUM

*Frieda's father, Rabbi
Nissan Stolzberg, zt"l*

סֶפֶר הָאָבִיב

הלק ראשון

על פרקי אבות

כולל שלשה ביאורים

א) פרחי האביב
ב) ועד חכמים
ג) תולדות חכמים

ובסוף הספר

קונטרס אושר הנצחי המדבר ממהות עוהיב
וקונטרס קלא רשופרא דרוש לראש השנה

אשר חברתי בעזרת החונן לאדם דעת

ניסן שטאלצבערג

SEFER HEAWIW
Komentar zu Pirke Awoth
Verlag des Verfassers:
Rabbiner Nüssen Stolzberg, Wien
20., Heinzelmanngasse Nr. 18/11
Druck: Appel & Co., Wien, 9., Liechtensteinstraße Nr. 21

1933 — תרצ"ג

נרפס בבימ"הרשום של המחים אפפעל, וינה, 9., רחוב ליכטנשטיין 21

*Title page of Rabbi Nissan Stolzberg's
book,* Sefer He'aviv, *a commentary on
Pirkei Avot (Vienna, Verfassers: 1933)*

167

Opa Shmuel Stolzberg (c. 1935)

Oma Blima Stolzberg (c. 1935)

Tante Regina (c. 1935)

Onkel Aaron (c. 1935)

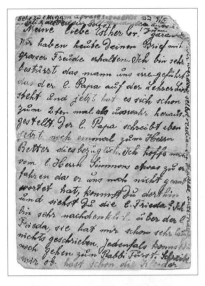

Frieda in England, 1939, with her first pair of "half-shoes"

Postcard from Mama Stolzberg in Yugoslavia to Frieda's sister Esther in England, 1940, lamenting the lack of mail from Frieda

Shefford, 1941: Group picture, students and staff

Shefford, 1941: Students and staff in the Hut

Postwar Sports Day: Frieda receiving sports prize from Rabbi Schonfeld (in uniform)

Shefford Summer Camp, 1944: Class taught by Meyer "Bubu" Eisemann. Frieda is the bored girl, third from the left.

Shefford Summer Camp, 1944: Tennis players surrounding
Meyer "Bubu" Eisemann. Frieda is at far left.

Frieda jumping hurdles on the Meadow, in Shefford, 1944

EXTRACT FROM PARLIAMENTARY DEBATE ON THE
EDUCATIONAL BILL, April 4th, 1944. *(Hansard, pp. 1972-1973)*
In Parliament the School received tribute in the course of the debate
on the Education Act:

Captain Sir Austin Hudson: "I want to try to get an undertaking from the Minister to bring in a school which is, I believe,
unique. It is the Jewish Secondary School . . . which has now been
evacuated . . . the Jewish community — it is the only higher school
of the Jewish community — want to rebuild it . . . when this school,
which is unique, is rebuilt after the war, it will be able if possible to
qualify for the 50 per cent grant. I can assure him that the members
of the Jewish community will find the other 50 per cent . . . It has an
excellent educational history behind it, with 90 per cent successes."

Mr. R. A. Butler (Minister of Education): ". . . I am aware
of the School and the excellent principles of the School, and would
not like to do anything to prejudice it in anyway, but would rather
encourage the Hon. Member and his friends. A School such as the
Hon. Member has in mind would under that provision be able to apply
for grant. . . . Sympathetic consideration will be given to any proposal
that may be put forward in regard to this School . . ."

An official "Extract of a Parliamentary Debate on the Educational Bill," April 4,
1944, in which tribute is paid to Rabbi Schonfeld's secondary school in Shefford

London hostel, 1945: (from left to right) Frieda, Pepi, Marga

*Frieda (on the right) and
Marga in London, 1945*

*Frieda arranging flowers
in the London hostel*

*Miss D. seated at her desk in the London hostel, 1945. A picture
of Rabbi Schonfeld takes pride of place.*

London hostel, 1945: (from left to right) Marga, Rita, Frieda, Edith

London hostel, 1945: top row (left to right): Dora, "Gypsy" (Bertha), unknown, Zelma. Seated (left to right): Rita, Frieda, Ruth

Signed photo of Rabbi Solomon Schonfeld, zt"l, wearing his silver-decorated tallit

Lag B'Omer outing, London, 1947. Frieda is second from the left in the second row.

At the seaside, 1946: seated (from left to right), Pepi,
Sonja, Frieda, Hedy; Marga is in front.

Passport photo of Frieda, age sixteen

From left to right, Frieda, Sonja, and Marga, in London hostel

Frieda in Israel, 1952, with cousins Mina, Aryeh, and baby Ilana

Cousin Mina

"Two Hundred Viennese Martyrs": A news report of the discovery in 1973 of the mass grave of 200 massacred Jews in Brko, Yugoslavia. Outlined in ink are the names of Nissan and "Eva" (Yocheved) Stolzberg (Frieda's parents), Oma Blima, and an unknown relative, "John Stolzberg."

HEBREW/YIDDISH TERMS

(Transliterated)

acharon, acharon chaviv	the last and the best
aliyah	immigration (lit. "going up") to Israel
bar (bas) mitzvah	boy's (girl's) assumption of adult religious responsibility
bentch/es/ed	saying /says/said the blessings after a meal
chalutz (im)	pioneer(s)
chazer (or *chazir*)	pig meat
chazer treif	nonkosher pig meat
Chevra Kadisha	burial society
Chumash (Chumashim)	Five Books of Moses (pl.)
chuppah	wedding canopy, wedding ceremony
daven, davening	to pray, praying
drashah (drashot)	sermon(s)
frum	devout

gonif	thief
goyim	gentiles
hachsharah	training for making aliyah
Haftarah	weekly reading from the Books of the Prophets
Haganah	Israel's pre-state defense force
Haggadah	order of prayers said at the Passover Seder
Halachah	Jewish law
Havdalah	prayer said as the Shabbat ends
horah	circle dancing
Kaddish	prayer said for the deceased
Kiddush	blessing over wine, said on Shabbos and holidays
kohen	priest
kugel	pudding
Lag B'Omer	holiday between Pesach and Shavuos
lashon hara	gossip or calumny
l'chaim	to life; a toast
lokshen	noodles
lokshen kugel	noodle pudding
ma'abarah	transit/absorption camp for new immigrants
mechitzah	wall or curtain separating between men and women
Mizrachi	Israeli political party
Motzi	blessing over bread
nigun (-im)	melody (pl.)
Nissan	a man's name; name of a Hebrew month

parashah	weekly portion, Torah reading
Pesach	Passover holiday
peyos	sidelocks
Rosh Hashanah	Jewish new year
semichah	rabbinical ordination
Shabbos, Shabbat	the Sabbath
sheitel	wig
Shema	Jewish Credo
shidduch	arranged match; match
shiksa(s)	gentile girl(s)
shiur (*shiurim*)	lesson(s)
shofar	ram's horn
shtiebel	small shul
siddur (*siddurim*)	prayer book(s)
simchah	joyous event
Sukkos	Festival of the Booths
sukkah	booth built to specifications for the festival
tallis, tallit	prayer shawl
Tanach	Bible
tefillin	phylacteries
treif	nonkosher
tzimmes	dish based on cooked carrots
Yediot Acharonot	Israeli newspaper
yichus	pedigree
Yiddishkeit	Judaism
zemiros	songs sung at the Sabbath table

ABOUT THE AUTHOR

Frieda Stolzberg Korobkin was born in Vienna into an Orthodox rabbinic family. In 1938, after Hitler's rise to power, Frieda's parents sent her and her three siblings to England on the *Kindertransport*. They never saw their parents again. In September 1939, at the outbreak of World War II, Frieda was evacuated to the English countryside, where she lived for several years with gentile families before joining Rabbi Solomon Schonfeld's Jewish school-in-evacuation for the last two years of the war.

Frieda has lived in England, Israel, and the United States. She has worked as a secretary, high-school English teacher, office manager, and freelance writer. She and her husband, entertainment attorney Leonard Korobkin, live in Los Angeles, California. They have three married children and many grandchildren.